KISS the COD

Superstitions, Traditions, Omens and Old Wives' Tales
of Atlantic Canada

Vernon Oickle

BLUE
BIKE
BOOKS

The Publisher: Blue Bike Books
Website: www.bluebikebooks.com

Library and Archives Canada Cataloguing in Publication

Oickle, Vernon, 1961–, author

    Kiss the cod : superstitions, traditions, omens and old wives' tales of Atlantic Canada / Vernon Oickle.

ISBN 978-1-926700-62-5 (pbk.)

    1. Superstition—Atlantic Provinces. 2. Folklore—Atlantic Provinces.
I. Title.

GR113.5.A8O535 2015   398'.4109715   C2015-900794-1

Project Director: Nicholle Carrière
Project Editor: Sheila Cooke
Cover Image: © Elena Elisseeva / Thinkstock
Illustrations: All illustrations are by Roger Garcia, Peter Tyler, Patrick Hénaff and Craig Howrie except: p. 12, Ihfgraphics; p. 15, d_rich; p. 18, Jupiterimages; and p. 202, EVRENSEL BARIS BERKANT all © Photos.com.

We acknowledge the financial support of the Government of Canada through the Canada Book Fund (CBF) for our publishing activities.

I✦I Canadian   Patrimoine
       Heritage   canadien

Produced with the assistance of the Government of Alberta, Alberta Media Fund.

PC: 30

DEDICATION

Dedicated to the memory of my grandmother, Pearle, and mother, Viola, the two women who inspired in me my interest in Maritime folklore and superstitions.

CONTENTS

ACKNOWLEDGEMENTS

Writing a book of this nature requires the support and trust of a lot of people. I say trust because the people of Atlantic Canada take their culture seriously, and they must be assured that their traditions will be in good hands. After writing several books dealing with Maritime folklore and traditions, I feel I have earned their trust, and I thank them for their continued faith in my efforts.

Two other important people in this process have been publisher Nicholle Carrière, who had sufficient faith in the project to give it the green light, and editor Sheila Cooke, who guided me through the painstaking process of revising and whipping the manuscript into shape. Thank you Nicholle and Sheila for your support.

PREFACE

Most times, it is difficult to tell where folklore ends and superstition begins. What is considered by some to be hard-earned wisdom or knowledge may be dismissed by others as worthless drivel. However, no matter how you define this collection, superstitions are, in effect, a holdover from an earlier, more innocent time—a time before modern science intervened to find a logical explanation for natural phenomena that, at times, had defied explanation.

While it is true that superstitions are beliefs that lack scientific proof, it is also true that such beliefs are part of our collective heritage. They are a valuable source of information from which we can learn a great deal about our ancestors. Today, we may see superstitions as nothing more than assumptions based on personal opinions, but earlier generations often used these beliefs to explain natural occurrences and, based on those beliefs, made decisions that impacted their lives and the lives of their families. For example, they would look to the sky and study the behaviour of animals, birds and insects for clues about what type of weather they should expect, and to know when to plant their gardens, milk their cows or make their hay. They would also recognize the signs regarding impending death or the birth of a child.

A superstition is the belief that one event causes another, without any physical process linking both events. For instance, it's a widely held belief that if a bird hits a window, it's a sign of impending death. Certain superstitions may be the result of real observations and may even have some truth to them, but they are not always taken seriously because they cannot be logically justified or explained. However, the fact remains that in Atlantic Canada, superstitions and old wives' tales, as they are affectionately known, are recognized and even embraced as an important part of the region's culture.

This book is a collection of such superstitions bits of wisdom found throughout Atlantic Canada that have been passed down from earlier generations. While this book is meant to be enjoyed, keep in mind that these superstitions have been around for many years, and as such, they provide an important link to the region's past. Enjoy!

About the Title

The tradition of "kissing the cod" began in Newfoundland many generations ago, and it continues to this day. It is part of a ceremony often used to welcome newcomers to the island and involves a codfish and a type of Newfoundland rum called Screech. For that reason, this ceremony is also referred to as a "Screech-in."

The ceremony is usually performed at pubs or other public places, but a local family may perform the ceremony. Tradition dictates that you must have a Newfoundlander present for the ceremony.

First, you must get your shot of Screech ready for consumption. Then you kiss the cod.

Once this task is finished, you must answer the question that's asked by the person performing the ceremony: "Is ye a Screecher?"

The reply to this is, "'Deed I is me old cock, and long may your big jib draw!" (Translation: "Yes indeed, my friend, and long may your big sail—i.e., jib—draw wind." Or, "May there always be wind in your sails.")

Afterwards, the shot of Screech must be consumed. At this time, the newcomer is officially accepted and welcomed as a Newfoundlander.

First Comes Love...

The quest for love and happiness has been at the forefront of human existence for centuries. In Atlantic Canada, if you're looking for love, you might want to pay close attention to the following superstitions.

IF AND WHEN

Candles and Horseshoes

☛ As many candles as are left on the birthday cake after you blow once, it will be that many years until you are married.

☛ The number of nails in the horseshoe you pick up will be the number of years until you are married.

Just Wait a Year

☞ If you fall upstairs, you will not be married for at least another year.

☞ If you look under the bed, you will not marry for another year.

☞ An unmarried girl may throw a shoe over her shoulder at the door. If the shoe lands with its toe pointing towards the door, then the girl will marry within a year; if not, she will have to wait at least another year.

Careful, Now

☞ Do not sweep a circle around a boy or girl, or he or she will never marry.

☞ If you look at the moon through a knothole, you will never be married.

☞ If an unmarried woman starts a quilt and doesn't finish it, she will never marry.

☞ Hope chests figure into the lore of many regions, including Atlantic Canada. A girl was to begin to collect personal items and clothing, as well as household linens and other items she planned on using in her married life. Once placed in the chest, they may not be tried on or used; otherwise, the woman would be condemned to spinsterhood.

Watch What You Eat

☞ Eat the point of a piece of pie first, and you will remain unmarried.

☛ If you take the last piece of bread off the plate when it is not offered, you will never be married; however, if you take it when it is offered, you will marry well.

☛ If an unmarried woman takes the last piece of anything, she will be an old maid unless she kisses the cook.

☛ If an unmarried woman finds two yolks in an egg, it means she will soon be married.

☛ If two forks are set mistakenly at a place setting on a table, the one who sits there will get married next. However, a single woman should never sit at the corner of a table, or she will never marry.

FIGURING OUT WHO

Peas in a Pod

☛ Finding nine peas in a pod is generally considered lucky, and in terms of love, if a single woman finds nine peas, it means she will soon marry. It was once believed that if a single woman who found nine peas in a pod put them on the trim above the front door, the next unmarried man to come through that door would be the one she should marry.

☛ A variation states that after she puts a pea pod with nine peas over the door, if a married man comes under it first, she will not be married within the year; if a single man first, she will be married within the year.

Love Apples

☛ If you twist the stem of an apple while also saying the letters of the alphabet, whatever letter you're on when the stem comes off will be the first letter in the name of your future spouse.

☛ A variation of this is if you are trying to decide between more than one love. Repeat their names in order as you twist the stem, and the name you're on when the stem falls off will be the person you will wed.

☛ To see an image of her future husband, a woman should eat an apple while sitting in front of a mirror and then brush her hair. An image of the man will appear over her shoulder.

☛ Remove the skin of an apple in one continuous peeling while thinking of your loved one and throw it over your shoulder. If the peeling breaks you will not see him, but if it remains whole, you will see him soon.

☛ Young women and men should wet as many apple seeds as for each of those they pine over, then name and toss them up toward the ceiling. The seed that sticks to the ceiling is the name of the one who loves you most.

☛ Press the seeds of an apple against your forehead; the number of those that do not fall off will tell you how many days it will be until you meet your one true love.

To See the Future

☛ Hang a wishbone over the front door, and the first man who passes under it is the man you will marry.

☛ If a woman finds a whole grain in the rye bread on three consecutive Fridays, then the first person she meets afterward will be her husband.

☛ Go into a vacant house, throw a ball of yarn and say, "I pull, who winds?" The one you are to marry will answer you.

☛ Put the letters of the alphabet in a pan of water under your bed. The next morning, the letter of your future husband will be turned over.

☛ Put a four-leaf clover in your Bible. The man you meet while you are carrying it will be your husband.

☛ Kiss a baby on the ninth day after its birth, and the next man you kiss will be your future husband.

☛ Walk backwards nine steps, and you will see the hair colour of the person you will marry.

☛ If you burn a match to the end, it will make the initial of the first name of the man you are to marry.

☛ It is said that if a young woman is blindfolded and led into the garden to pull up a cabbage in the fall, she will learn about the kind of man she will marry. If the root of the cabbage is straight, then she will marry a handsome man, but if it is crooked, then he will be ugly. If there is a large amount of dirt on the root, he will be a man of wealth.

☛ If you throw coins into a wishing well during a full moon, you will see the face of your true love reflected in the water below.

☛ If a woman stands by a well and makes a wish, it is supposed to come true. In the olden times she usually wished for a husband and children and then dropped in her coin. If she saw her own reflection, her wish was bound to come true.

Housekeeping Happiness

☛ A woman who cannot wash dishes without splashing her clothing will find she ends up with a drunkard for a husband.

☞ If a young woman has dirty elbows, then she will marry a poor man.

☞ If a woman cannot make a good fire, she will not get a good husband.

Man's Best Friend

☞ If a dog follows a woman home, it is bringing the spirit of a man she will shortly meet.

☞ Anyone fond of dogs will make a good marriage partner.

The Man of Her Dreams

☞ If a girl drinks salty water and then goes to sleep, she will dream about her future husband.

☞ Sleep with the Bible under your pillow for three nights in a row, and you will dream of your future husband.

Spring Fever

☛ Go fishing on the first day of May. If you get a bite, it means you will soon meet your beau. If you get a catch, it means you will get a husband within the year.

☛ Look in a well on the first day of May to see the face of your future husband.

☛ If you walk around a wheat field on the first day of May, you will meet your mate.

☛ On the first day of May before sunrise, a maiden should go into the garden and search for a snail. If she finds one within a shell, her future husband will have a house. If the first snail she sees is outside its shell, her husband will be poor. If she then sprinkles sand in front of the snail, the sand will form the initial of the man she is to marry.

☛ If a young woman wishes to see the face of the man she will marry, on the first of May, she should hold a mirror face down over a clear stream; she will see the reflection of her one true love.

DID YOU KNOW?

If a couple first catches sight of each other in a mirror, they will have a happy marriage.

Body Language

☛ If the lines on the palm of a woman's hand form an "M," she will marry a man with money.

☛ If a woman has hairy legs, she will marry into wealth.

Which One Shall I Marry?

☞ Before you go to bed, name the corners of your bedroom. The first corner you look at in the morning will indicate which of the four persons named loves you best.

☞ Place chestnuts in a fire and name them for the loves in your life. The nut that jumps first signifies which man loves you most.

☞ Put three holly leaves under your pillow at night, and name each leaf. The one that is turned over in the morning will be your husband.

HE LOVES ME,
HE LOVES ME NOT

Young women looking for assurance in love are heard to recite the phrase, "He loves me, he loves me not," as they hold a daisy and carefully pull off one petal at a time. If a woman is lucky, she will have chosen a daisy with an odd number of petals, and the flower will affirm the love of the man she longs for. This common practice was actually passed down from one gypsy generation to the next. Gypsies also believed that a young woman could find her true love by sleeping with daisy root under her pillow.

Does He Love Me?

- ☞ Put a spoonful of pepper on a cold stove lid, then a spoonful of salt, and name your beau out loud. Now light a fire under that lid. If the one you have named truly loves you, the pepper and salt will blaze up and burn.

- ☞ It is a commonly held belief that if, while putting on her favourite necklace, a woman speaks the name of the man she hopes to marry, that wish will come true. However, if the clasp breaks and the necklace falls off, then the marriage is doomed to failure.

- ☞ If you are able, with one breath, to blow off all the seeds from a dandelion seed ball, your sweetheart loves you.

- ☞ Name an eyelash for your lover and blow it away. If you never see the eyelash again, then you are truly loved.

- ☞ If you can make a fire that burns, your sweetheart or husband loves you. But, if the fire does not burn well or goes out, you are not loved or are being cheated upon.

☞ If you light a match, put it down and it burns up entirely, you are loved. Or, in a variation, light a match and let it burn as close as possible to your fingers, then spit on the burnt part and hold the match by the head. If it burns up entirely, without breaking, your beau loves you.

☞ If you put on your stockings wrong side out, your sweetheart loves you.

DID YOU KNOW?

If a male and female both reach for the same thing, while eating, at the same time, a romance is brewing.

Is He True?

☞ Cut a lemon in half and rub both pieces on the four posts of your bed, then put the two halves under your pillow. If you dream of your beau or husband, he is faithful; if you do not dream of him, he has been unfaithful.

☞ It is said that if a woman burns her biscuits in the oven, then her one true love is angry with her. If she burns her bread, her one true love has been unfaithful.

☞ If you burn your tongue on a hot liquid, it means your spouse is cheating on you.

☞ If a woman in love dreams of a cat, it means that her lover is true.

☞ If a woman loses her garter on the street, it means her husband or boyfriend has been unfaithful.

☞ Name a worm with your sweetheart's name while fishing, then bait your hook with it. If you catch a fish with that worm, he or she is true to you.

Always on my Mind

☛ If you have a burning on your left ear, it indicates that you are in your lover's thoughts.

☛ If your eye quivers, then your lover is thinking about you.

☛ If a girl's cheeks burn for no reason, then her lover is talking about her.

☛ A young woman's lover is thinking about her if her apron becomes unfastened and drops off.

☛ If a girl upsets coffee, water or any drink, her sweetheart is thinking of her.

☛ If a girl's shoelace comes untied, it signifies that her beau is thinking about her.

Yes or No?

☛ If a woman receives a proposal she is not certain she should accept, she should take some hairs from a cat, fold them in a piece of paper and place it under her door stoop. In the morning, the hairs should have formed themselves in either an "N" or a "Y," and she will have her answer. If you throw pennies into running water at the time of your engagement, you will have good luck in your marriage.

DID YOU  KNOW?

Two lovers will never agree once they're married if both of them wipe their faces on the same towel.

WHEN WILL I SEE YOU AGAIN?

Signs from Within

☞ If you accidentally drop the comb while combing your hair, you will see your sweetheart before your hair gets mussed again.

☞ The girl who cuts her fingernails on Saturday will see her sweetheart on Sunday.

DID YOU KNOW?

If you stub your toe, kiss your thumb and face the opposite direction—you will see your sweetheart. Or, in another version, if you stub your toe, walk backwards over the spot where it happened, turn around three times clockwise, then kiss your thumb—you will see the face of your true love.

Signs Around the House

☞ If you drop a dishrag, it is a sign that your lover will come to you soon.

☞ If a pot or pan falls and lands upside-down on the floor, you will soon see someone you love.

☞ A tablespoon dropping to the floor is a sign that your lover is coming.

☞ If you find a pin facing towards you, pick it up and you will see your beau that day.

☛ If you spit on a piece of burning wood that falls from the fire and name it for your sweetheart, then replace it on the fire, your love will arrive before the flames consume the wood.

Signs in Nature

☛ To hear the call of a hawk means that your beau is approaching.

☛ Seeing a redbird on Saturday morning means your sweetheart will visit you soon.

☛ As soon as you see the first robin of spring, sit down and remove your left stocking. If it contains a hair, your beau will soon call upon you.

☛ A toad crossing the road in front of you indicates that you will see your sweetheart that day.

☛ The girl who finds a one-leafed clover will receive a letter from her sweetheart. A girl who finds a four-leafed clover will meet her lover on that day.

...Then Comes Marriage...

You've found love, so now what? Getting married in Atlantic Canada is a complex business of avoiding bad luck and courting good luck.

SETTING THE DATE

Choose a Month

☞ June, October and December are the luckiest months for a wedding—particularly June. Couples who marry in the month of June will find happiness and prosperity, and June brides are said to be more fertile.

Marry in Lent, you'll live to repent.

Choose a Day

☞ A bride and groom should never be married on either of their birthdays. It is bad luck. It is also bad luck to marry a person born in the same month as you.

☞ It is considered bad luck to be married on a Friday in the month of May.

☞ If there is a full moon one to two days before the wedding, then your married life will be filled with luck and good fortune. Another version says it is good luck to marry on the day of a full moon.

☞ Although many couples now tie the knot on the weekend, traditionally, Wednesday was the day that promised matrimonial bliss. It was actually once considered bad luck to marry on Saturday.

Married on Monday, married in health;
Married on Sunday, married for wealth.

Choose a Time

☞ Marry while the hands of the clock go up, and you will succeed in life.

DID YOU KNOW?

It is bad luck to postpone a wedding.

BRIDAL WEAR

Don't Tempt Fate

☛ A bride should never try on the entire wedding outfit and gown before the day. This was thought to be tempting fate and the spirits to interfere in the wedding.

☛ No one should try on the wedding rings before the ceremony because doing so will bring bad luck to the marriage.

☛ Wedding linens were marked with the bride's maiden name rather than her married initials so as not to tempt the fates to interfere by anticipating the event.

DID YOU KNOW?

It is bad luck for a bride to practice signing her new name until it is legally hers.

Something old, something new,
Something borrowed, something blue,
And a silver sixpence in your shoe.

The Dress

☞ Tradition says that the bride should never make her own gown, but that a happily married woman with children should sew it so that the married woman's luck will be passed on to the bride through the sewing.

☞ The final stitch of the wedding gown should not be completed until the bride is departing for the church. This is to fool the spirits into believing that the wedding is still a ways off.

☞ If a bride drops a pair of scissors while working on her wedding gown, it means her fiancé has been unfaithful.

☞ The colour of the wedding gown is said to foretell the future happiness of a marriage:

Married in white, you have chosen right;
Married in red, you'd better be dead;
Married in yellow, ashamed of the fellow;
Married in blue, your lover is true;
Married in green, ashamed to be seen;
Married in black, you'll ride in a hack;
Married in pearl, you'll live in a whirl;
Married in pink, your spirits will sink;
Married in brown, you'll live out of town.

The Veil

☞ Veils were once used to mask the identity of the woman until the ceremony was complete. If another man was in love with the bride, he wouldn't be able to kidnap her for himself. Some cultures used the veil to hide the bride's face to ward off bad luck.

☞ A bride should always wear a veil to protect her from evil.

☞ If anyone should see the bride's veil before the wedding, her married life will be unhappy.

The Garter

☞ A garter worn by a bride on her wedding day brings good luck. Decades ago, it was believed that if a grooms-man pulled off the bride's garters just before she entered the bedroom, good luck would also be passed on to him. To make the removal easier and less embarrassing for the bride, ribbon streamers were often attached to the garters. This custom later evolved into the removal of the garter by the groom, who would then throw it (backwards and over the right shoulder) to all the unmarried men at the wedding. Whoever caught it got to wear the garter on his hat for the rest of the day and would be the next to marry.

☞ If a bride wears another girl's garter during the wedding, that girl will also be married within the year.

THE WEDDING DAY

Nice Day for a Wedding

☛ If the bride burns a pair of her old shoes the night before the wedding, it will not rain on her wedding day.

☛ If it rains on your wedding day, it is a sign that you will shed many tears during your married life. However, if you choose to go with a different version, rain on your wedding day means you will have many children.

☛ It is a good sign to see a rainbow on the day of your wedding.

DID YOU KNOW?

It is good luck for a cat to sneeze near the bride on her wedding day.

Getting Dressed

☛ To awaken the bride on her wedding morning is bad luck. Let her sleep as long as she will.

☛ To ensure a long and happy marriage, when getting dressed for the wedding, the bride should always put on her right shoe first. If a bride puts on her left shoe first, her married life will be unhappy.

☛ It is good luck for the bride to find a spider in her wedding gown when she is putting it on.

☛ It is held that a final look in the mirror right before the bride leaves her home for the ceremony will bring good luck. However, if she looks in a mirror again before the ceremony, her luck will tarnish to bad.

☞ It is bad luck for anyone other than the bride to wear white on the wedding day.

DID YOU KNOW?

If a kettle of hot water is poured over the doorstep of the home in which the bride is getting ready, there will be another wedding in that house within the year.

Going to the Chapel

☞ It is considered bad luck for the groom to see the bride before the ceremony on the wedding day.

☞ Walking is thought to be the best way of getting to church because there are more chances of spotting lucky animal omens, including a lamb, frog, spider, grey horse or black cat.

☞ Bad animal omens include seeing a pig, a hare or a lizard running across the road, or hearing a crow after dawn on the morning of the wedding.

☞ Seeing a chimney sweep on the way to the church means the bride and groom's good luck will last throughout the year. In fact, there was once a tradition of making sure that a chimney sweep met the bridal couple on their wedding day.

☞ Should a bride or groom encounter an open grave on their way to the chapel, it is considered a foreboding sign of something terrible in their future.

DID YOU KNOW?

Coming home from church can be equally hazardous. Tradition dictates the new wife must enter her new home by the main door and, to avoid bad luck, must not trip or fall—hence the custom that a bride should be carried over the threshold.

The Ceremony

☛ The bride should step into the church with her right foot first to ensure good luck.

☛ During and following the wedding ceremony, it is customary for the bride to take the groom's left arm, thus leaving the groom's right arm free to protect his new wife.

☛ If the sun shines on the bride during the wedding ceremony, the couple will be blessed with a long, happy marriage.

☛ If the groom drops the wedding ring, the marriage is doomed to fail.

☛ It is bad luck for a bat to appear during the wedding ceremony.

☛ If matrimonial candles are lit during a wedding, and they sputter out, it means an evil spirit is nearby. As long as the matrimonial candles burn bright, the couple will have a long and happy life together.

☛ Having the bride and groom jump over a broom handle during the ceremony ensures that they will have a long, happy life together.

☛ In many countries, following the ceremony, the bride had to kiss all the men present to assure her marital happiness. Another custom found in many countries is that the bride must cry the first the groom kisses her, or she will cry all of her married life. In modern times, however, the kiss at the end of the ceremony symbolizes that the marriage vows have now been sealed.

☛ It is bad luck for anyone to walk between the bride and groom once the wedding vows have been exchanged. If the new bond is broken, the couple is destined to break up, and divorce is imminent.

The Send-off: Rice and Shoes

☞ If you throw rice at the bride and groom following the ceremony, they will be blessed with many children. The tradition of throwing rice comes from the ancient Hindus and Chinese, for whom rice symbolizes fertility.

☞ Another reason for throwing rice at a wedding comes from the belief that evil spirits hovered near all weddings. The rice was thrown as food for the spirits to keep them occupied and away from the happy couple, of whom they were extremely jealous.

☞ Eating rice or other grains at a wedding symbolizes health, wealth and happiness for the newly married couple.

DID YOU  KNOW?

Wreaths of corn or wheat traditionally decorated the church because they were also symbols of fertility and were considered to be a blessing upon the marriage.

☞ Old shoes are tied to the back of the wedding car to symbolize the couple starting out on a new journey together. This custom comes from a time when guests would throw shoes at the bride and groom, believing that the couple would have great luck if the shoes hit either them or their carriage.

☞ In Anglo-Saxon times, the bride was symbolically struck with a shoe by her husband during the wedding ceremony to establish his authority over her.

☛ Brides used to throw a shoe at their bridesmaids; whomever the shoe hit was considered to be the next one to be married. Thankfully, this tradition has evolved into the throwing of the bouquet.

DID YOU KNOW?

A week before the wedding, it is considered good luck to have a cat eat out of the bride's left shoe.

Bridesmaids

☛ The tradition of bridesmaids evolved from the custom of surrounding the bride with other richly dressed women in order to confuse evil spirits. In many places, the bride would not put on her wedding dress until she was in the protective confines of the church.

☛ Another possible reason for bridesmaids is because of an old Roman law requiring 10 witnesses at the wedding dressed as the bride and groom to outwit the evil spirits attending happy events and to confuse the Devil so he would not know who was getting married.

☛ If a bridesmaid holds the bride's dress on her lap for 10 minutes before the bride puts it on, she will be a bride within the year.

☛ If a bridesmaid is older than the bride, she should wear something green or else she may never marry.

☛ Any bridesmaid that carries a piece of the wedding cake in her pocket until the bride and groom's honeymoon is over will marry soon.

The Wedding Cake

☛ It is bad luck for a bride to bake her own wedding cake.

☛ If a bride tastes the wedding cake before it is cut, she will lose her husband's love.

☛ If a bride saves a piece of her wedding cake, she ensures that her husband will be forever faithful.

☛ The top layer of the wedding cake should be frozen after the wedding and then thawed on the first anniversary to rekindle the romance.

DID YOU KNOW?

If a single woman sleeps with a piece of wedding cake under her pillow, she will dream of the man she will someday marry.

HAPPILY EVER AFTER

Newlyweds

☞ It is bad luck for a bride to put her bare feet on the floor on the night of the wedding.

☞ The honeymoon tradition is rooted in the past when the groom captured a bride from her family. The couple hid while the moon passed through its phases. During this time, it was hoped the woman would become pregnant, in which case her family would want her to remain with her husband. To encourage fertility and to increase the chance of a male child, the couple drank honey wine or mead (a drink brewed with honey).

☛ The first gift the bride opens should be the first gift she uses.

☛ If a young bride bites into an apple and finds a worm, it means she will be blessed with lots of babies.

Married Life

☛ As long as you keep some of the bread of your first wedded meal, you will never be in want.

☛ If a bride breaks her wedding ring, it means she will soon be a widow.

☛ If either a husband or wife loses their wedding ring, the couple will soon separate.

☛ It is bad luck for a husband or wife to give their spouse a watch because it's a sign they will soon break up.

DID YOU  KNOW?

Dreaming of clover means you will have a very happy and prosperous marriage.

He who is needy when married,
will be rich when buried.

...Then Comes Baby

*Like everything else in Atlantic Canada, having a baby
comes with its own share of superstitions.*

EXPECTANT SUPERSTITIONS

DID YOU  KNOW?

To boost their odds of conceiving, women will often carry around a lucky rabbit's foot. It makes sense—rabbits seem to have no trouble reproducing.

Boy or Girl?

☞ To predict the sex of a baby, take a pin, needle or wedding ring and attach it to a thread or strand of hair. Hold the dangling item over the pregnant woman's belly while she is lying down. If the needle or wedding ring swings in a strong circular motion, she will be having a boy. If it swings like a pendulum, the baby is a girl. An alternate version of this baby gender prediction method is to dangle the needle or wedding ring over the expectant mom's wrist instead of the belly.

☛ It is believed that if a pregnant woman has a great deal of back pain, then she will give birth to a boy.

☛ It is said that if a pregnant woman carries her baby all out in front, she will have a boy. Conversely, if she carries the baby weight more evenly or side to side, it will be a girl.

☛ If an expectant mother is carrying her baby low, it is a boy. Conversely, if she is carrying the baby high, it is a girl.

More Baby Predictions

☛ It is said that if a woman suffers from heartburn while she is pregnant, the baby will be born with a full head of hair.

☛ It was believed that if a woman was burned during her pregnancy, her baby would be born with a birthmark in the exact location of the burn.

☛ If a pregnant woman finds two yolks in an egg, it means she will give birth to twins.

DID YOU KNOW?

If you dream of fish, it means someone you know is pregnant.

Pregnancy Don'ts

☛ It was considered bad luck for a pregnant woman to go outside during a solar eclipse because it would cause the baby to born with a deformity. To be safe, pregnant women were always kept inside.

☛ It is considered bad luck for a pregnant woman to cross her legs.

☛ It is said that pregnant women should not attend funerals.

☛ It is bad luck to allow a pregnant woman to walk up or down a set of stairs without assistance.

☛ It is bad luck to prepare a room for a baby or to buy baby clothes during pregnancy. Wait until the baby is born to avoid jinxing anything.

BABY TALK

Birthday Destiny

Superstitious people will tell you that the day of the week on which you are born will determine the kind of person you are.

- Sunday: You tend to be optimistic and positive. Good luck tends to follow you. You should wear gold to improve your fortunes.

- Monday: You tend to have an active imagination. Generally, people like to be around you. Silver is your good luck charm.

- Tuesday: If you are born on this day, red is your colour. You tend to be enthusiastic about life. You have an ability to influence others.

- Wednesday: Blue brings you good luck. You tend to get along well with other people. You do not like to argue.

- Thursday: You love travel and discovering new places. You tend to be carefree. The sign of the cross will bring you good luck.

- Friday: You tend to fall in love easily. Success will follow you throughout your life. Diamonds will bring you good luck.

- Saturday: You are not afraid of hard work. You tend to be more content with your life. Like those born on Sunday, gold will bring you good luck.

Monday's child is fair of face;
Tuesday's child is full of grace;
Wednesday's child is full of woe;
Thursday's child has far to go;
Friday's child is loving and giving;
Saturday's child works hard for a living;
But the child born on the Sabbath is
lucky, bonny, wise and gay.

☛ It was believed that babies born in the morning sunshine would live longer than those born later in the day.

☛ Babies born at sunrise will be more successful in life than those born at sunset.

DID YOU KNOW?

Opal is the birthstone for anyone born in October, but it is bad luck for anyone other than people born in October to wear an opal.

Baby Pronouncements

☛ A very old superstition from the region was to tell the bees if a new baby was born in the family. When you hear of the birth, you should go to the nearest door to the outside and call out the news joyfully to the bees. In turn, the bees are said to deliver the message to the gods of fortune, and your baby will be blessed throughout its lifetime.

☞ If you rub money on a baby's head, he or she will be rich in the future.

☞ Babies born with red hair are born with good luck.

☞ It is bad luck for your baby to have his or her hair cut before their first birthday.

☞ It is bad luck to let a baby look at itself in a mirror before he or she is a year old.

☞ It is good luck for a baby to pee on you.

☞ It is good luck to kiss a baby on the forehead.

☞ Never step over a crawling baby or you will stunt its growth.

☞ Never tickle the bottom of baby's feet because it is said to make him or her stutter when they get older.

☞ Keep cats away from babies because it is said they "suck the breath" of the child.

☞ Placing a Bible under your baby's pillow will keep away evil spirits.

Birthday Celebrations

☛ It is bad luck to celebrate your birthday before the actual date of your birth; if you do, it might mean that you will not celebrate another birthday.

☛ When you're turning 40, you should try to avoid anyone who might wish you a happy birthday because it is believed that receiving congratulations for your 40th birthday means bad luck for the rest of your life. Some people will try to avoid friends and may not leave their house for several days before, on and after their birthday. In some regions, many people do not celebrate their birthday after the age of 30.

Listen to Your Body Talk

People in Atlantic Canada believe that when your body talks, you should listen. Everything from your hair colour to the lines of your palm to having an itchy nose has meaning.

SEEING RED

It may be good luck to be born with red hair, but for whatever reason, in Atlantic Canada, redheads tend to get picked on more than most in the superstition department—Anne of Green Gables notwithstanding.

Personality Defects

☞ Red hair signifies a person who is very passionate and hasty, very suspicious and extremely jealous.

☞ Red hair almost always indicates that a person is dishonest.

☞ It is said that a man with red hair is cunning, deceitful and cannot be trusted.

☞ It is said that redheaded women are either violent or false, usually both.

☞ Red hair is the sign of a vixen.

☞ It is bad luck to have the eye of a red-haired woman rest on you.

☞ It was once thought that a woman with long red hair had a loose tongue and was likely to spread gossip.

Personal Misfortune

☞ It's felt that red-haired people don't make good butter, for the butter always has a slight tang to it.

☞ It's a widely held belief that bees will sting redheads more than people with any other colour hair.

Stay Away

☞ It is believed that much sorrow will come to those who associate with redheads.

☞ There is an old belief that if you meet a redhead in the street, you should spit, turn around and quickly walk away because it is considered bad luck to pass someone with red hair.

- Never lodge at red-haired people's houses, for these be folks to dread.

- Do not let the shadow of a red-headed person fall upon you, or it will bring you bad luck.

It's Not All Bad to be Red...

- It was believed that red hair denotes a person of sharp wit, easily agitated and unforgiving, but once a friend, a true one.

- If a person has red hair on the top of his head or the back of the neck, then he will be wealthy.

- It is considered lucky to rub your hand on the head of a redhead.

For Non-Redheads

As we've seen, red hair can be both a curse and a blessing. What do the other hair colours say about someone's personality?

- Brown hair means trustworthy.

- Black hair means evil tendencies.

- Balding or bald men are said to be more virile.

- White or grey hair means wisdom and experience.

DID YOU  KNOW?

If you pull out a grey or white hair, 10 more will grow in its place.

SIGN LANGUAGE

Would You Say That to my Face?

☛ If your ears are burning, there is someone talking about you.

☛ If you hear a ringing in your ears, it means someone is talking about you.

☛ If your left ear itches, it is said that someone is saying something bad about you. Conversely, if the right ear itches, then it is believed that someone is saying something good about you.

☛ If you bite your tongue, someone is talking badly about you. Bite your sleeve to make them stop. Biting your tongue can also mean you are going to kiss a fool. If you bite your tongue while talking, it means you have recently told a lie.

☛ If your nose itches, it means someone is thinking about you, or it might also mean that you are going to kiss a fool, see a stranger, be in danger or receive some bad news. Still others will tell you that it means you will be invited to a party, or that someone you haven't seen in a while will soon visit.

Rich or Poor?

☛ If your left hand itches, you're going to be rich. To make this prophecy come true, you should spit in your palm then rub your hand on your left bum cheek. If your right hand itches, you're going to be poor.

☞ Depending upon where you are in the region, there are different versions of these beliefs. For instance: if the palm of your right hand itches, you are going to shake hands with a stranger. Or, if the palm of your right hand itches, it means you will soon be paying out money.

Spooky
☞ If the bottom of your feet itch, it means somebody has been walking over the ground that will someday be your

grave. It might also mean that you are soon going to walk on strange ground.

☛ If you get a sudden chill, it means someone just walked over the ground under which you will be buried.

☛ If your left eyelid twitches, it is believed that you are soon going to hear about a tragic death in the family.

☛ It was once thought that people whose eyebrows had grown together were evil.

☛ People with two different coloured eyes were once said to be witches.

☛ People with hiccups were once thought to be possessed by the Devil. Others took a less dire view, believing that having hiccups simply meant that someone, somewhere, was talking badly about you.

How Romantic

☛ A dimple on your chin means you have been kissed by Cupid.

☛ If there is a fever blister on someone's lips, it is a sign that they have been kissed.

☛ A white spot on a woman's little fingernail reveals that she has a sweetheart.

☛ The number of Xs in the palm of your hand tells you the number of children you will have.

☛ When your upper lip itches, it means you will soon kiss someone.

Clumsy

☞ If you stumble with your right leg and your birthday is on an odd day, or if you stumble with your left leg and your birthday is on an even day, then that means you are going to have good luck. However, if you stumble with your right leg and your birthday is on an even day, or if you stumble with your left leg and your birthday is on an odd day, that means bad luck is coming.

☞ If you stub your little toe, you will soon take a trip.

DID YOU KNOW?

If your feet ache, then it is going to rain.

The End is Nigh

How will you know when it's time to meet your maker?
What should you do for someone who has just passed on?
Read on for superstitions regarding all things death.

DEATH AND DYING

Nothing generates more superstitions in the Atlantic region than the certainty of death and dying.

Easing the Passage

☛ When a sick person is on his or her death bed, animals should be kept out of the room because otherwise, it is believed that upon death, the person's spirit will enter the body of the animal.

☛ All windows and doors should be opened at the moment of death so that the soul can leave. The soul of a dying person can't escape the body and go to heaven if any doors in the house are locked.

☛ The eyes of the dead must always be closed, or they will find someone to take with them.

☛ If you kiss the deceased, it sends them into the afterlife without any regrets.

☛ You will have bad luck if you do not stop the clock in the room where someone has died.

☛ Mirrors in a house with a corpse should be covered, or the person who sees himself will die next.

☛ If you touch a loved one who has died, you won't have dreams about them. Similarly, it is a commonly held belief that if you touch the deceased before the burial, you will not grieve for them.

The Funeral

☛ If a woman is buried in black, she will return to haunt the family.

☛ Funerals on Friday foretell another death in the family within the year.

☞ It is bad luck to wear new clothes to funeral but especially bad luck to wear new shoes because the soul of the deceased will get angry and haunt you.

☞ It's bad luck to meet a funeral procession head on.

☞ Pointing at a funeral procession will cause you to die within the month.

☞ It is not only disrespectful but also bad luck to count the number of cars in a funeral procession.

☞ Breaking into a funeral procession is bad luck.

☞ It is bad luck to point at a cemetery or a grave.

☞ Seeing a crow at the gravesite is a good sign.

☞ You should never stand in direct sunlight at a funeral, or you will be the next one to die.

☞ When at a cemetery, never walk on a grave for fear of disturbing the dead.

☞ Thunder following a funeral means that the dead person's soul has reached heaven.

☞ If the person buried lived a good life, flowers will grow on the grave. If the person was evil, weeds will grow on the grave.

DID YOU  KNOW?

People in the Town of Lunenburg, Nova Scotia, like in most other early settlements, used to hold funerals from their homes. But did you know that they used to make one window in their homes larger than the others to allow coffins to pass through?

More Cemetery Superstitions

☞ Many people believe it is best to avoid passing a cemetery on the way to church.

☞ Hold your breath while going past a cemetery, or you will breathe in the spirit of someone who has recently died.

☞ Never pick a flower from a grave and throw it away because the place where it falls will become haunted, and you will have bad luck.

☞ You should tuck your thumbs into your fists when you pass a cemetery to protect your family from death.

Haunted

☞ An empty rocking chair rocking on its own in the house could be a harbinger of death or perhaps a sign that a ghost is visiting and has been around for some time.

- ☛ If a door slams shut for no obvious reason, it means someone in the afterlife is trying to get your attention.

- ☛ Small lights dancing and hovering in mid-air are called "orbs," and they are the spirits of the deceased.

DID YOU KNOW?

Every year, on the night of November 1, light candles for each deceased relative and place them in the window in the room where the death occurred. This will keep their spirits from haunting you.

SIGNS OF DEATH TO COME

With death being an ever-present certainty, it's no wonder that a superstitious lot such as Atlantic Canadians sees death omens in the most commonplace occurrences.

Nature Calls

☞ If a bat flies around a house three times, it is a death omen.

☞ A beetle walking over a person's shoe is an omen of death.

☞ If a bird hits a window, it means someone close to you is going to die. In a variation of this superstition, it is believed that the window must break before it's considered bad luck. Similarly, if a bird gets into the house, it's a sign that a death in the family is imminent.

☞ The discovery of a dead bird on the ground is a harbinger of an impending tragedy.

Dogs howling in the dark of night,
Howl for death before daylight.

Dark Dreams

☞ Dreaming of flowers is a sign that you will soon attend a funeral. Similarly, it is said that if you imagine you can smell flowers, it is an omen of death.

- Dreaming of a woman in white is a sign of impending tragedy.

- If you dream you are falling, it's a sign of death.

- Most Atlantic Canadians believe that if you dream of death, it means there will be birth in your family, but if you dream of a birth, it means there will soon be a death. However, others believe that dreaming of the dead means someone close to you is going to die. Still others believe that if you dream of someone who is dead, then you will hear from a long-lost friend or family member you haven't seen in many years.

DID YOU  KNOW?

If you have a bad dream and you tell someone about it before you have breakfast (or in some regions, brush your teeth), then that dream will come true.

Household Harbingers

- If a clock that has not been working suddenly chimes, there will be a death in the family.

- If a mirror in the house falls and breaks by itself, it's said that is sign that someone in the house will die soon.

- If a window in your home suddenly slams shut on its own, someone is going to die.

- If a picture falls off your wall, it's a sign of death in your family.

- If you hear three knocks at your door, but there is no one there, that's called a token and it means someone in your family is going to die.

- If there comes four knocks on the outside of your house, one on each outer wall, it means there will be a death in the family.

- Placing a hat on a bed is the ultimate in bad luck symbols. It means someone you know will soon die.

- Dropping an umbrella on the floor means that there will be a death in the house.

- If a pot falls to the floor, it means someone in the home will soon die.

HEED THE WARNING

Warnings about imminent death come in all forms, but one of the most common, and one many people believe you should take seriously, is the forerunner.

Death Foretold

If you see a vision of someone who isn't there, that's called a forerunner, and it's a sign of imminent death for someone you care about such as a family member or a close friend. Atlantic Canadian legends are rife with stories of these harbingers of impending disaster to our loved ones.

My superstitious family takes these forerunners very seriously. My mother, like many of my female ancestors before her, was "tuned in," as they called it, and she paid serious heed to these warnings. Many times I heard my mother and grandmother talk about "seeing" people before they died even though there was no physical presence. Each of these stories would cause a shiver to race up my spine.

My mother told me of a happening one Saturday afternoon some years ago when several members of the family were sitting around the kitchen table at the old family home, enjoying a friendly game of cards. She looked up and noticed the figure of a man pass by the window. It was quick, but several others saw him as well. All heard the door handle jiggle and the latch lift three times as if someone was about to enter. No one came in. Everyone agreed that they had just seen a forerunner. Although they had no idea who was about to die, they feared it would likely be someone within the family. The card game immediately ended; no one felt like playing anymore.

Lo and behold, three days later, one of my mother's favourite uncles suddenly dropped dead of a heart attack. Everyone who had been present for the card game that preceding Saturday concluded that it was the uncle's forerunner they had seen. It's the stuff of family legend, but this is the nature of a forerunner.

Around the House

*In Atlantic Canada, just about everything that happens
in your home has special meaning.*

HEARTH AND HOME

Burning Superstitions

☞ Placing grain dipped in Holy Water around your house is said to protect it from burning down.

☞ If a fire hisses while it is burning, misfortune is about to strike someone in the household.

☞ If sparks are generated by a fire, the person in whose direction those sparks fly will soon receive some good news.

☞ Never have candles in your house unless they've been lit. It's bad luck. It is also bad luck to blow out a candle; instead, it is best to put out the flame with your fingers.

Moving Day

☞ When you move into a new house, it is good luck to bring a new broom and a loaf of bread with you.

☞ Never take an old broom with you to your new house.

☞ It is good luck to bring salt into your new house.

IN THE KITCHEN

One of the most superstitious places you'll find in any Atlantic Canadian home is the kitchen. There you'll find a long list of old wives' tales.

Kitchen Karma

☞ It is very bad luck to ask, "What could go wrong?" in a kitchen.

☞ Keeping a cup of vinegar in the kitchen is good luck.

☞ It is bad luck to leave your oven empty. Use it as a place to store your pots.

☞ It is bad luck to sing or whistle at the kitchen table. One outcome for doing it anyway was that you would be poor for the rest of your life. Another was that the singing invited the Devil to dinner.

☞ Never leave empty bottles sitting on your dinner table because it allows them to be filled up with bad luck.

☞ Dropping your dishcloth on the floor means a stranger will soon visit your home.

☞ If you drop a plate and it breaks, don't fret; that's said to be good luck. However, if it lands upside down and doesn't break, you can expect bad luck.

☞ If you drop a glass and it breaks, expect bad luck. But if it doesn't break, then it means an angel is watching over you.

☞ You should anticipate bad weather if you spill a glass of water in the kitchen.

☞ It is bad luck to hold a cup while filling it; you should always set it down first. Also, never fill a mug by pouring the liquid over the handle, or someone you know will soon die.

DID YOU KNOW?

If you choke while taking a drink of water, it means someone is thinking of you. Of course, others will say that it means you told a lie or stole something.

Consequential Utensils

☞ Never accept a utensil from another person once you have taken your place at the dinner table, or expect bad luck if you do.

☞ It is bad luck to spin your knife at the dinner table.

☞ Some people will tell you never to leave an empty place setting at your table, lest you invite the Devil to eat with you. Others will say that setting an extra place at the dinner table will invite the friendly spirits to stay for a meal.

☞ It is bad luck to give another person a knife as a gift; when you do, it cuts your friendship. If you do give someone a knife, include a penny to blunt the edge.

☞ If someone sharpens your knife you must pay them, or you will cut yourself when you use it next.

☞ Never hand someone else a knife; it is bad luck. Lay it down and let them pick it up.

☞ Dropping any utensil can mean different things depending on what it is and where you are in the region. For instance, some people say that dropping a knife is bad luck; dropping a fork means someone is going to visit; and dropping a spoon means the visitor will be someone you haven't seen for some time. Elsewhere, if you drop a knife, a man will visit your house; if you drop a fork, that visitor will be a woman; and if you drop a spoon, you can expect that visitor to be a child.

Knife falls, gentleman calls,
Fork falls, lady calls.
Spoon falls, baby squalls.

Tea Time

☛ If you forget to put the cover on the teapot, it's a sure sign that someone will visit.

☛ Let a teakettle boil, and you chase away all your friends.

☛ Some people will tell you it is a good omen if a tea bag breaks open in your cup; others say to expect bad luck if your tea bag breaks open in your cup. Specifically, when a tea bag breaks, you can expect one of four outcomes: ill health; going to take a trip; going to come into money; or someone you know is going to die.

Baking All the Rules

☛ Burning bread means you and your family will go hungry some day.

☛ Never bake bread after sunset, or it won't rise.

☛ To place the sign of the cross upon a freshly-baked loaf of bread is said to bring good luck to the household and keep evil spirits at bay.

☛ To avoid misfortune in the household, you must slice a baguette diagonally in the same direction as the scores on it.

☛ Never cut a new loaf of bread on both ends. It's bad luck.

☛ To cut bread in an uneven manner is a sign that you have been telling lies.

☛ If you burn a slice of toast, you will hear from a member of your family you have not seen in a while.

☛ It is bad luck to drop a slice of bread butter side down.

☛ A loaf of bread should never be turned upside down once it's cut, or it will bring bad luck.

☛ A loaf of bread always had to be right side up in the breadbox. If the loaf was placed upside down, it meant bad luck for vessels leaving port and symbolized a cap-sized vessel.

☛ Never sweep breadcrumbs onto the floor, or you'll sweep away a friendship. Or, another version of this superstition has it that if you brush crumbs from the table to the floor, you will always be poor.

☛ A cake baked in the afternoon will fall with the setting sun.

☛ A cake will fall in the middle if more than one person stirs it.

DID YOU KNOW?

Never make fudge on a wet day, or it will fail every time.

What's Cooking?

☞ When peeling onions, always start at the root end to avoid shedding any tears. Others say that if you chew gum while cutting up onions, you won't shed a tear.

☞ Always leave the pot lid on when you're cooking vegetables that grow on top of the ground. If not, they'll always burn.

☞ Never discard the wishbone from a turkey. Allow it to dry on the windowsill for one week. Once the wishbone is dried, two people, using their pinky fingers, should grasp either side of the bone and pull it apart while making a wish. The person who ends up with the larger piece will have their wish come true.

☞ If gravy turns out lumpy, it means bad luck. In another version, lumpy gravy means a storm is brewing.

☞ Never pass the pepper directly to someone, or you will hate each other for the rest of your lives.

☞ Burning your potatoes is a sign that someone in the family is going to be ill.

☞ If your pot of potatoes boils dry, it's a sign of a major rainfall.

☞ If your pot boils dry while you are cooking eggs, it means a bad storm is coming.

☛ When cooking eggs, put a drop of vinegar in your water to prevent the shells from cracking. If an eggshell does crack while it is boiling, you should expect a visitor to your home.

DID YOU KNOW?

Some people believe that if you've been visiting at someone's home for several days and your host serves carrots for dinner, then he or she is trying to tell you that you have overstayed your welcome and that perhaps it is time for you to leave.

Here's Salt in Your Eye

Many cooks in Atlantic Canada have a habit of tossing salt over their left shoulder, but they do it for good reason, especially if they spill salt.

According to local superstition, it is bad luck to spill salt. If you do, simply throw a bit of salt over your left shoulder—doing so will blind the Devil and ward off the bad luck he was intending to bring to you.

Leonardo da Vinci's *Last Supper* has given us two common superstitions: the first is that spilling salt brings bad luck, and the second is that you should never seat 13 at dinner. In fact, if you look closely at da Vinci's painting, you can see that Judas has knocked the saltcellar over with his elbow. Thanks to Judas Iscariot, spilled salt is associated with treachery and lies.

DID YOU KNOW?

☞ It is bad luck to knock over a saltshaker, but did you know that spilling the pepper means that you will soon have an argument?

☞ Salty soup means the cook is in love.

HOUSEHOLD CHORES

People in Atlantic Canada are especially superstitious when it comes to everyday household chores.

Sweepstakes

☞ Picking up a broom that has fallen over will give you good luck.

☞ It is bad luck to carry a broom over your shoulder.

☞ It is bad luck to pass a broom through an open window.

☞ Stepping over a broom is bad luck.

☞ Misfortune will find you if you lean a broom against a bed.

☞ It is unlucky to borrow a broom.

☞ Always sweep the dirt out the back door and not the front, or you will sweep away your friends. Another version has it that if you sweep the dirt from your house through an open door, you also sweep away all your good luck.

☞ If someone is sweeping the floor and sweeps over your feet, you'll never get married. A more serious version of this superstition states that sweeping over someone's feet will sweep their life away. You can "undo" the curse by biting the end of the broomstick.

☞ If you drop your broom in front of the door, then you will have a visitor that day. If you don't want a visitor to come back, sweep out the room after he or she leaves.

☞ It is bad luck to sweep between sunset and sunrise. For instance, sweeping your floor after sunset will cause someone at sea to drown, and if you empty your dustpan after dark, you'll throw away a friendship. A more harmless effect of night-time sweeping is that it will bring a stranger to visit.

Sew What?

☞ To upset a box of pins foretells a surprise as long as some of them are left in the box. If they all spill out, there will be no surprise.

☞ Stabbing your knitting needles through your balls of yarn will bring bad luck to anyone who wears something made from that yarn.

☞ Never pass a needle directly from one person to another; it is bad luck. Always stick it in a piece of fabric and pass it along that way.

☞ If you drop a needle, count to three for good luck before picking it up.

☞ Although it hurts, some say it is good luck to prick yourself while sewing.

☞ When darning a sock, always turn it inside out for good luck.

☞ When you are sewing and your thread knots and tangles, someone is talking about you.

☞ If you break your needle while making a dress, you will live to wear it out.

☞ It is bad luck to sew or mend clothing while someone is wearing it unless the person in the clothes holds a thread in their mouth. In particular, never sew a button on a shirt while it is being worn.

☞ Similarly, if you mend your apron or dress while you are wearing it, someone will lie about you, or some other bad luck will befall you.

☞ Never start a garment on Friday unless you can finish it the same day.

☞ Never begin to make a dress on Saturday, or the wearer will die within the year.

☞ Never sew on Sunday because you will have to rip out all of those stitches when you get to heaven.

Cut It Out

☛ Dropping a pair of scissors is said to warn that a lover is unfaithful.

☛ Breaking one blade of a pair of scissors is an omen of quarrelling and discord; if both blades are broken at once; a calamity is to be feared.

☛ Scissors should always be purchased; they should never be given as a gift.

☛ It is bad luck to pass a scissors from one person to another point end first.

Laundry Lore

☛ It is bad luck to do the laundry on Saturday and Tuesday.

☛ Hang socks on the clothesline so that toes are facing toward the house, or it's a sign that someone will be walking away.

☛ If you hang up a man's socks by the toes, money will slip through your fingers.

☛ Changing the sheets on a bed on Friday will bring bad dreams.

☛ Never turn your mattress on a Sunday, or you'll have bad dreams.

On You and In You

Everyone knows that what you wear and what you eat makes a statement about you, but sometimes things just happen by chance.

DRESS FOR SUCCESS

In Atlantic Canada, even the clothes you wear and the way you get dressed can come with their own superstitions.

Getting Dressed

☞ When you put on new clothes for the first time, you should make a wish.

☞ It is unlucky to get dressed by putting on your shirt with the left arm first, or pants with the left leg first or shoes with the left foot. Always start with the right side of your body to ensure that you have a good day.

☞ It is good luck if you accidentally put your sweater on inside out, but you must wear it all day for the charm to work. If you change it, you will have bad luck your whole day.

☞ Missing a button hole while buttoning up your shirt is considered bad luck.

☞ Always button your shirt from the neck down.

☞ It is good luck to wear a sock with a hole in it.

☞ Wearing odd socks is bad luck.

Women's Wear

☞ It is said to be bad luck to wear anything white after Labour Day.

☞ If a girl's skirt turns up at the bottom, it means her lover is in a bar.

☞ Women should never wear pearls; they will bring disappointment.

☞ If you accidentally tear a hole in a new dress the first time wearing it, don't fret; you will have a new one before that one is worn out.

Outerwear

☞ If you drop a glove, it is unlucky for you to pick it up. You should ask someone else to get it for you.

☞ It is bad luck to wear a hat in the kitchen or while sitting at the dinner table.

DID YOU KNOW?

When a girl places a man's hat on her head, it means she desires a kiss.

☞ It is bad luck to put shoes on a table, counter, chair or bed. Putting new shoes on a table is especially bad because new shoes were put on the dead, who were traditionally laid out on the table.

☞ You should not leave your shoes with the toes towards the door because this orientation suggests that you be leaving the house in a hurry, most likely because something bad has happened.

☞ It is bad luck to leave footwear upside down with the soles facing up. If you see shoes or slippers turned over, you will quarrel with someone close to you.

☞ It is good luck to tie your old shoes together and then to hang them from a nail.

☞ Never give shoes for a gift, as it will cause the person who receives the gift to walk away from you.

☞ If your new shoes squeak when you walk, it means that you haven't paid for them yet, but if your old shoes squeak, it is considered good luck.

☞ Holes in the bottom your shoes signal that you're going to get some money.

☞ If a lace breaks while tying your shoe, it is considered good luck. To improve those chances of good luck, carry the broken lace around with you in your pocket.

☞ If you tie someone else's shoelaces, make a wish as you're doing so.

☞ If your shoelace comes undone, that means you are about to take a trip. However, you should be cautious as it could mean you might encounter a run of bad luck on that trip.

FOOD FOR THOUGHT

They say that you are what you eat. If that's the case, then you should pay attention to what you eat in Atlantic Canada.

Health Food

- If you eat one apple a day, you will be blessed with good health. Remember the old saying: an apple a day keeps the doctor away.

- Eating a tablespoon of honey every day will also keep you healthy.

- Eating blueberries will help you keep your youth.

- Eat fish to improve your brainpower.

- Eating carrots will improve your eyesight.

- Cabbage is good for helping you lose weight.

- Parsley or fresh mint will cure bad breath.

- Eating onions will put hair on your chest.

- Liver will make you more fertile.

- Oysters and peanuts are aphrodisiacs.

DID YOU KNOW?

It is bad luck to eat the seeds of an apple.

☞ When eating a fish, you should begin at the tail and work towards the head. This will bring you good health and good luck.

☞ Always bury fish bones for good luck.

Walking on Egg Shells

☞ Some early settlers told their children that witches lived in eggshells and that they made boats out of them that they would sail out onto the ocean to cast spells upon the fishermen. The children were told that when they ate an egg, they should push their spoon through the bottom in the form of a cross before discarding the shell.

☞ Breaking up empty eggshells will bring you good luck.

Egg-ceptional

☛ Eating eggs will help prevent wrinkles.

☛ Eating at least one egg a day will improve a man's virility.

☛ Eating the eggs laid by a white hen was said to cure stomach pains and headaches.

☛ At least once a year, infants were given hard-boiled eggs dyed red (the blood of Christ) to keep them healthy for the coming year.

You're Yolking

☛ Finding a black spot on a yolk is an omen of bad luck.

☛ Finding an egg with no yolk at all means a terrible tragedy is about to strike.

☛ It is considered good luck to find two egg yolks within one shell.

Here's to Your Health

Throughout Atlantic Canada, you'll find a wide variety of superstitions relating to health. For example, it is a widely held belief that if you pee on side of the road, you will develop a sty on your eye. So it should go without saying that if you want to avoid getting a sty, don't pee in the ditch. There are many other superstitions surrounding every kind of malady, especially relating to the pervasive common cold.

COLD WAR

Preventive Action

☛ If you catch a falling leaf on the first day of autumn, you will not catch a cold for the remainder of the winter.

☛ If you go outside with wet hair, you will catch a cold. You should wait at least half an hour or until your hair dries.

☛ Eating oranges will prevent the common cold.

☛ Feed a cold, starve a fever.

Bless You

☛ Place a hand in front of your mouth when sneezing—your soul may escape otherwise. Cover your mouth when you yawn for the same reason.

- When someone sneezes, you should say "God bless you" because at one time it was believed that the Devil entered your mouth when you opened it to sneeze. In some cultures, it was even considered a sin to sneeze. Others believed that your heart momentarily stopped during a sneeze, and saying "God bless you" was a way of welcoming the person who sneezed back to life.

- It is bad luck to sneeze to the left.

- Looking directly at the sun will cause you to sneeze.

- If the person you are talking to sneezes after you tell them something, then it means they believe what you told them is true.

Sneeze on a Monday, you sneeze for danger;
Sneeze on a Tuesday, you will kiss a stranger;
Sneeze on Wednesday, you sneeze for a letter;
Sneeze on Thursday, you sneeze for the better;
Sneeze on Friday, you sneeze for sorrow;
Sneeze on Saturday, you will see your beau tomorrow;
Sneeze on Sunday, and bad luck will follow you all week.

RANDOM NUGGETS OF WISDOM

The common cold is not the only thing you can take steps to avoid. The following is some conventional wisdom, often dispensed by Dr. Mom.

Listen to Your Mother

- ☞ It is widely believed that handling a toad will give you warts.

- ☞ If you have shingles and they circle your waist, you will die.

- ☞ Never have a haircut in March, or you will have a headache for the remainder of the year.

☛ If you step on a crack, you will break your mother's back.

☛ Corn on the cob will give you diarrhea. If you don't eat bread with corn on the cob, you will throw a fit.

☛ Don't let children eat candy because the sugar will make them hyperactive.

☛ If you don't wait an hour after a meal to go swimming, you will get cramps and drown.

☛ Always cover your head in cold weather to keep your body from losing heat.

☛ If you pull your fingers and crack your knuckles, you will get arthritis.

☛ If you swallow gum, it will take seven years to digest.

☛ Reading in low light will make you go blind.

Home Remedies

While some of Atlantic Canada's folk medicines do not fall into the category of superstition, others definitely do. Their origins are diverse, and we can trace customs from continental Europe, England, Ireland, Scotland and the Channel Islands, and from First Nations sources on this side of the Atlantic. For example, the use of maggots in a poultice and the curative properties of seashells are a direct influence of First Nations, and some old-time remedies in which herbs and balsams hold primary place indicate cultural knowledge of medicinal properties of native plants.

EVERYDAY CURE-ALLS

Common table salt and baking soda had many uses in Atlantic Canadian medicine. Vinegar (mostly apple cider or white vinegar, though any type would suffice) also had many uses in local folk medicine. Peppermint tea, grogs and water from the last spring snow were once believed to cure all manner of ailments. Blackstrap molasses was used as a spring blood tonic throughout many areas of Atlantic Canada because of its rich iron and other mineral contents. Honey not only tastes great, but it also heals bee stings and other cuts, and soothes sore throats. Women use it on their faces. And many people in Atlantic Canada believe that dumping honey down a well will keep the water pure.

One other prevalent cure-all in Atlantic Canada, but particularly Prince Edward Island, is the potato. For example, if you have a cold or the flu, simply fast from all processed foods and eat boiled potatoes with carrots, onions, celery and parsley. The potato industry is a big business in PEI. Recent studies confirm that the industry is worth over a billion dollars to that island's economy each year. Potatoes are the primary cash crop on the island, and PEI continues to be the largest potato-producing province in Canada, growing one-quarter of the potatoes in the country. While potatoes fuel the province's economy, the famous root vegetable can also be used in dozens of cases of sickness or injury, as you'll see if you read on.

There are many other substances used throughout the region for medicinal purposes. Check out these "cures" if you dare, but be warned, before you try any treatment, you should always seek the advice of a medical practitioner.

ACHES AND PAINS

Headache

☞ Walk backwards, around in a circle, preferably.

☞ Rub peppermint oil on your forehead, temples or back of the neck. Garlic is also said to work.

☞ Take a hot shower.

☞ Rub a mixture of cow dung and molasses on your temples.

☞ Put leeches on your forehead.

☞ Wrap damp cloths around your head and burn scented wood.

☞ Lean your head against a tree and have someone else drive a nail into the opposite side of the tree.

Earache

☞ Dilute vinegar with water and squirt the mixture into your ear. Or inject several drops of apple cider vinegar into the sore ear.

☞ Warm up some oil (olive is the best choice) and put several drops into your ear.

Toothache

Many of us may remember when our mothers would fill a sock with salt, sew it shut, heat it in the oven or on the old wood stove, and use it as a salt pack to treat toothache or a swollen jaw due to an infected tooth. We'd take the heated sock to bed with us, sleeping with it against our cheek.

☞ Vinegar left in the mouth will provide relief.

☞ Cut a slice or wedge of lemon and bite into it if you can to release some of the juice.

☞ Slice a fresh piece of cucumber and hold it over the sore area. Or mash a piece of cucumber with a bit of salt and pack it around the sore tooth.

☞ Make a paste with cayenne pepper and water. Then apply it directly to the sore tooth.

☞ Wet the tip of your finger with water and dip it in baking soda; then apply to the sore tooth.

☞ Dissolve a heaping spoonful of baking soda in a small glass of lukewarm to warm water; then swish the mixture around in your mouth.

☞ Pebbles from the grave of a pious person provided a faith cure for a toothache. Retrieve several stones from the grave, and as long as you possess the stones, your tooth-ache will be gone. Lose the stones, and your pain will return.

☞ Add a few drops of tea tree oil to a small glass of luke-warm to warm water and rinse your mouth with it.

☞ Mix half a teaspoon of salt in a glass of very warm water and use it to rinse your mouth thoroughly. Repeat as often as needed.

☞ Put one teaspoon of dried peppermint leaves in a cup of boiling water and steep for 20 minutes. After the liquid cools, swish it around in your mouth. Repeat as often as needed.

☞ Chew on fresh peppermint leaves.

☞ Chew on a fresh piece of ginger.

☞ Place a warm, wet tea bag on the tooth.

☞ Swish a bit of rye whisky, scotch, brandy or vodka in your mouth.

☞ Saturate a cotton swab or cloth with vanilla extract and hold in place over the affected tooth. If you don't have vanilla extract, try almond extract, peppermint extract or lemon extract.

☞ Soak a cotton ball with apple cider vinegar and hold it in place.

☞ Cut a fresh piece of potato (raw, skin off) and hold in place. Or pound a piece of raw potato, mix in a bit of salt and use the mash.

☞ Place a piece of tobacco on the tooth.

☞ Put pine balsam on the aching tooth.

☞ Mix equal amounts of salt and pepper with a few drops of water to form a paste. Apply the paste directly to the affected tooth and allow it to sit for a few minutes. Do this daily for several days.

☞ At the first sign of a toothache, chew raw onion for a few minutes to relieve pain. Or place a piece of raw onion directly on the bad tooth or gum.

☞ Crush one clove of fresh garlic and mix with some table salt or black salt and apply it directly to the affected tooth to alleviate the pain. Or chew on one or two cloves of garlic to get relief.

☞ Grind two cloves of garlic and mix in a little olive oil or any vegetable oil. Now apply this solution to the affected tooth.

☛ Dab some clove oil directly on the sore tooth. Or mix a few drops of clove oil in a small glass of water and use it as a mouth rinse, being sure to swish it over the sore tooth as much as possible.

Sore Eyes

☛ Mix the ash of burnt tobacco into the water from May snow and bathe the eyes with the mixture.

Pain in the Side

☛ Put a pebble under the tongue.

Stomach Ache

☛ Eat the eggs laid by a white hen.

☛ Eat several whole cherries.

☛ Crush some willow bark into a fine powder and mix with water, then drink the mixture.

☛ Mix a little salt into a glass of water and drink it.

☛ Sip a cup of peppermint tea.

☛ As with a headache, walk backwards around in a circle.

☛ Ground and boiled juniper was supposed to be a panacea for stomach ills, as was dogberry extract and the extract from boiled alder buds.

☛ Mix some cumin seeds and coriander leaf juice with a glass of water and add a pinch of salt, then drink the mixture.

Rheumatism/Arthritis/Sore Joints and Muscles

☛ The great brown jellyfish was bottled, and when dissolved into a liquid, was rubbed on the affected parts to act as a counter-irritant. Be warned: this cure has a powerfully offensive odour.

☛ People with rheumatic tendencies wore an amulet of haddock fin around their neck, which acted as a charm against disease.

☛ To cure arthritis, wear a copper bracelet.

☛ Carrying the knot from a birch tree in your pocket will reduce joint pain.

☛ Chew on a piece of willow bark to relieve joint pain, particularly in the knees, back, hips, and neck.

☛ Boil a potato, wrap it up in a clean cloth, and apply it to those aching muscles. For a cold compress, refrigerate the boiled potato.

☛ Drink half a cup of pickle juice every day until the aches and pains are gone.

☛ Heat one cup of fresh water until warm, but not hot. Stir in a tablespoon of blackstrap molasses. Drink one cup of the mixture every day.

☛ Drink a cup of white willow tea twice a day.

☛ Crush several fresh peppermint leaves and add to water. Drink once a day.

☛ Drink a cup of juniper berry tea twice a day.

☛ Place one cup of golden raisins in a shallow dish, and pour in enough gin to just barely cover them. Cover with a towel and store them away in a dark place until the gin has evaporated—about two weeks. Once the gin is gone, eat nine of the raisins every day.

☛ Mix two tablespoons of cayenne pepper with half a cup of butter, and apply the paste directly to the sore joint.

☛ Mix half a teaspoon of cayenne pepper with one cup of apple cider vinegar, and soak sore hands or feet for 20 minutes.

☛ Although the hairs of stinging nettle are usually painful to the touch, when placed over a painful area of the body, they will reduce pain.

☛ Drink a cup of rose hip tea.

☛ Drink a cup of turmeric or ginger tea once a day.

☛ Rub a slice of onion over the bothersome area.

☛ Add two cups of Epsom salts to a tub full of warm water and soak in it for at least 15 minutes.

☛ Eat a bowl of uncooked spinach.

☛ Eat a handful of nuts.

☛ Rub a bit of olive oil onto your sore joints twice a day, massaging it into each one gently.

☛ Drink tea made from dandelion leaves, or throw a handful of fresh dandelion leaves into a salad.

☛ Cooked beets will help to treat arthritis.

☛ For a charley horse, plant your feet on a cold surface to remove the cramps, or apply a cold compress.

DIGESTIVE COMPLAINTS

Indigestion

☞ Chew some gum from a spruce tree.

☞ Mix a teaspoon of baking soda into a glass of water and then drink.

☞ Mix two teaspoons each of lime juice, ginger and honey into a glass of warm water; drink the mixture after your meal.

☞ Peel and eat a raw potato as you would an apple.

☞ Drink freshly squeezed potato juice first thing in the morning and after meals.

☞ Mix equal amounts of garlic and soya oil, and massage onto your stomach. Allow the oil to be absorbed by the skin.

☞ Mix two teaspoons of coriander, one teaspoon of ginger, three whole cloves and a pinch of cardamom in a glass of water, and drink the mixture.

☞ Place an ice bag on your troubled stomach for at least half an hour after meals to ease the pain.

☞ Grind several dried mint leaves into a powder and mix with a cup of tea.

☞ Drink buttermilk after every meal to prevent indigestion.

Hiccups

- Count to 10 while drinking a glass of water without stopping.

- Drink water while looking in a mirror.

- Take a drink of water while standing on your head.

- Have someone scare you.

- Breathe into a paper bag while counting to 10.

- Take a deep breath and hold it as long as possible without letting any air out, then exhale gently in a controlled way.

- Raise your arms above your head and hold your breath while you count to 10.

☞ Mix half a teaspoon of mustard seeds with half a teaspoon of ghee (clarified butter), and swallow the mixture.

☞ Swallow a teaspoonful of vinegar.

☞ Put one teaspoon of honey, stirred in warm water, on the back of your tongue, and swallow it.

☞ Slowly chew a teaspoon of dill seeds.

☞ Mix some lemon juice with water and then drink the mixture.

☞ Take a teaspoon of sugar and allow it to dissolve slowly in your mouth without chewing it.

☞ Drink a mixture of sugar and water.

☞ Mix one cup of milk with a teaspoon of salt; stir it until the salt dissolves completely. Drink the milk slowly.

☞ Boil one and a half cups of water and add a teaspoon of freshly ground cardamom. Allow the liquid to cool; strain the liquid and drink.

Hiccup Prevention

☞ Grind up watermelon seeds and sprinkle over your food.

☞ Crush four or five Indian gooseberries to extract the juice. Mix two teaspoons of the juice with one teaspoon of honey. Swallow this mixture every day.

☞ Mix one-half teaspoon each of onion juice and honey. Take it twice a day for one to two weeks.

☞ Eat two teaspoons of honey before breakfast every morning.

☞ Mix one teaspoon each of honey and ginger juice with two teaspoons of cumin seed powder. Eat it twice a day.

☞ Mix basil juice and honey in equal amounts and swallow it on an empty stomach daily.

☞ Drink a few ounces of potato tea every day.

Constipation

☞ Mix two teaspoons of dried dandelion leaves into a cup of hot water. Cover and let steep for about 10 minutes, then drink the tea. Do this up to three times a day.

☞ Eat unpeeled boiled potatoes or drink the juice to soothe inflamed tissue and provide bulk to the stool.

Diarrhea

☞ Brew some mint with water and make a tea to sip.

☞ Add a teaspoon of peppermint extract to a glass of warm water and drink.

☞ Drink flat ginger ale and eat a slice of dry burnt toast.

☞ Eat a slice of raw pumpkin.

☞ Eat unsalted potatoes mashed with water.

☞ Crush up a portion of blueberry root, mix with water and drink the mixture.

☞ Make a soup with blueberries. Dried blueberries are said to work better, but fresh blueberries will also work.

INJURIES

Burns

☛ Cut a slice of raw potato and rub it on the burn. Make sure the juice from the potato is released over the area. Or make a compress using cold, grated raw potatoes and apply to the burn. If not cold, mix with ice.

☛ Spread cold molasses on a burn until it stays in place, then rinse with cold water. If the molasses continues to run, it means there is still heat in the burn.

☛ Combine three or four tea bags, two cups of fresh mint leaves and four cups of boiling water. Strain liquid into a jar and allow to cool before using. Dab the mixture on burned skin with a cotton ball or washcloth.

Cuts

☛ Mix castor oil with lime juice and apply to the wound.

☛ If you don't have access to soap and water, then you should lick your wound to remove surface contaminants, but be sure to follow up with a soap and water as soon as possible.

Stopping Blood

☛ Apply a mixture of cobwebs and turpentine.

Nosebleed

☛ A nosebleed could be stopped by certain people who recited a secret prayer or rite to achieve the desired effect.

☛ Drill a hole in a nutmeg seed, and wear it around your neck on a string. If a whole nutmeg seed isn't available, two tablespoons of ground nutmeg sewn into a small cheesecloth bag could be substituted.

Infection

Many people of Newfoundland recall an old resident of their community who was regarded as remarkable in healing festered sores. It was generally some motherly old lady who did the doctoring.

☛ Some of the ingredients of a good poultice include scorched linen, burnt cream, the white of an egg, powdered dust of seashells, dried and powdered seaweed, goose grease and mouldy bread. The poultice is then placed over the sore. Or apply the paste directly to the infected area.

☛ Place raw bacon over the infected area and wrap with a bandage. Leave overnight.

☛ Put live maggots on the inflamed wound or sore, and let them go to work.

☛ Place a hot tea bag on the infected area, and keep it there until it cools off.

☛ Mix softened soap with sugar and make a paste to put on the infected area.

☛ Use a bread poultice to draw out the infection.

☛ Apply fresh pine gum to the affected area.

☛ Boil the root of a juniper tree, and once it is soft, mash into a paste and apply to the infected area.

CHRONIC COMPLAINTS

Insomnia

☞ Mix one tablespoon of honey into a cup of tea or warm milk for a relaxing pre-sleep drink.

☞ Dab a bit of lavender oil onto your temples and forehead before you hit the pillow.

☞ Put a drop of jasmine oil on each wrist just before you go to bed.

☞ Make a warm compress using grated raw potatoes and warm water. Place the paste in a cloth and secure it to your forehead before going to bed.

High Blood Pressure

☞ Add beets to your daily diet.

☞ Eat more bananas, lemons and spinach.

☞ Eat boiled potatoes, including the skins.

☞ Chew one or two raw garlic cloves every day.

☞ Eat one medium-sized, raw onion every day.

☞ Mix five or six drops of garlic juice in four teaspoons of water, and take it twice a day.

Hernia

☞ An old custom to cure a child of hernia was to split a green witch-hazel tree and pass the child through it.

Hemorrhoids

☛ Steep some horse chestnut in a tea and drink at least twice a day.

☛ Apply apple cider vinegar directly to the hemorrhoids, or add half a cup of it to your bathwater and soak in the tub.

☛ Eat oranges, grapefruit or lemons.

☛ Apply witch-hazel extract using a clean cotton swab or clean cloth.

☛ Mix lady's mantle in a cup of warm water, and apply directly to the hemorrhoids several times a day.

☛ Apply pine tar to the hemorrhoids.

☛ Crush several pieces of garlic and mix with warm water, then use as an enema.

☛ Rub turpentine directly on the inflamed area. Be warned: this will burn when it's applied.

☛ Steep a teaspoon of dried leaves from butcher's broom (or box holly) in a cup of tea and mix in a teaspoon of honey, then drink.

☛ Place a warm, moist tea bag on the hemorrhoids.

☛ Grind bayberry, goldenseal root, myrrh and white oak into a paste and apply directly to the hemorrhoids.

The Power of a Potato Diet

☛ Diabetes: Those with diabetes must have a steady supply of complex carbohydrates, but not in excessive quantities, to avoid creating too much sugar in the blood. On a potato diet, diabetics can lose weight without any harmful side effects.

☛ Gout: Gout is mainly caused by consuming too much meat and animal fat. One of the symptoms is the over-production of uric acid. The most important part of treatment is a diet low in this acid. Potatoes contain very little uric acid and can be the main ingredient in an anti-gout diet.

☛ Kidney Problems: To avoid having to resort to dialysis, people with kidney failure must eat little, but high-quality, protein. Potatoes fit the bill. Potatoes are excellent for urinary tract infection as well because they alkalize the mucous membranes to force bacteria to be passed out in the urine.

☛ High Blood Pressure: When certain bodily functions are disturbed, the kidneys excrete insufficient sodium, which leads to raised blood pressure (hypertension). Sufferers are prescribed an extremely low-sodium diet. This means eating foods such as potatoes that are naturally low in sodium and avoiding or restricting the use of salt in their preparation.

☛ Celiac Disease: While doctors say there is no cure for this grain intolerance, people with this condition find potatoes easy to digest.

COLD AND FLU

Sore Throat

☛ Pour one cup of boiling water over two teaspoons of dried raspberry leaves. Steep for 10 minutes and then strain. Allow to the mixture to cool, and then gargle with the liquid.

☛ Mix one teaspoon of sage in one cup of boiling water. Steep for 10 minutes, then strain. Add one teaspoon each of cider vinegar and honey; gargle four times a day.

☛ Mix one cup of hot water with half a teaspoon of turmeric and half a teaspoon of salt. Gargle with the mixture.

☛ Mix one tablespoon each of honey and vinegar (preferably apple cider vinegar) in one cup of hot water. Sip slowly while the liquid is hot.

☛ Mix one tablespoon each of honey and lemon juice in one cup of warm water and sip slowly.

☛ Mix one teaspoon of salt, half a cup of cider vinegar and one cup warm water. Gargle every 15 minutes as necessary.

☛ Combine one tablespoon of pure horseradish or horseradish root with one teaspoon of honey and one teaspoon of ground cloves. Mix in a glass of warm water and drink slowly.

☛ Sit with your face over a bowl of steaming hot water and your head covered with a towel to keep the steam in. Add one to two drops of eucalyptus oil.

☛ Make a compress by placing hot, mashed, unpeeled, boiled potatoes in a linen or cotton cloth, and apply to the throat.

☞ Rub a mixture of kerosene and butter on your throat and chest.

☞ Rub some honey on your throat and chest.

☞ Rub goose grease on your throat and wrap it with a towel.

☞ Make a paste by crushing raw onions, and then rub the paste on your throat and chest.

☞ Gum extracted from a pine tree and applied to the throat is said to work.

☞ Take the red pulp from a sumac tree, boil it in water and then gargle with the mixture.

☞ Boil some licorice root with water to make licorice tea. Strain and drink it to soothe your sore throat.

☞ Boil a cup of water, add one teaspoon of slippery elm herb and let it steep, covered, for at least half an hour. Strain and drink the mixture.

☞ Boil a cup of water, add one tablespoon of dried marsh mallow root and let it steep, covered, for at least half an hour. Strain and drink the mixture.

☞ Boil one litre of water and add one cup of honeysuckle flowers. Cover and steep for at least 10 minutes. Strain and drink the mixture.

☞ Drink a cup of basil, ginger and peppercorn tea three or four times a day.

☞ Drink a cup of tea made with lemon, apple cider vinegar, cayenne pepper and honey three or four times a day.

☞ Drink a glass of cinnamon and honey milk or tea.

☞ Gargle with warm salt water.

☛ Combine ground dried sage and echinacea and add water. Put that mixture in a spray bottle and use two puffs every couple of hours. Or make a peppermint spray using freshly ground peppermint in water to use whenever your throat feels sore.

☛ Tie a piece of salt herring around your throat at bedtime, and leave it there all night.

Cough and Congestion

☛ Mix kerosene with molasses and drink—this is not recommended today, popular as it was in yesteryear.

☛ Another effective home remedy for a stubborn cough was once extract of wild cherry mixed with spirits of turpentine.

☛ Some people used to drink a mixture of turpentine and spider webs to cure a chest infection.

☛ Snake root was steeped as a tea for a cough medicine.

☛ Drink a cup of rose hip tea.

☛ Lower your face to basin or bucket full of hot, steaming water and drape a towel over your head to trap the steam. Breathe in the steam to relieve congestion.

☛ Slather your chest and back with a thick coating of goose grease then place a layer of flannel over the grease. Do this before going to bed, and leave it on all night.

☛ Cook some onions until soft, then mix with molasses and eat. (Note: Some people substitute molasses with brown sugar.)

☛ Fry several onions and put them in a pillowcase. Pin the pillowcase around your neck at bedtime to allow the moist heat to rest on your chest and the fumes to penetrate your sinuses to clear up congestion.

☛ Apply a mustard plaster to your chest.

☛ Eat some horseradish to clear nasal congestion.

Fever
☛ Put sulphur in your shoes two or three times a day for several days.

☛ Put raw sliced potatoes on your forehead.

☛ Peel and remove the core of several apples. Slice the apples and add them to boiling water and then simmer until they are mushy. Strain and add two tablespoons honey. Drink the mixture several times a day.

☞ Cut an onion in half and place the pieces under the bed.

☞ Slice up a raw onion, put the pieces into a pair of socks and then put on the socks.

☞ If you prefer garlic over onion, slice up a clove of garlic and put the pieces in a pair of socks before putting them on.

☞ Make a "tea" by steeping sheep droppings, and then drink the liquid.

☞ Before going to bed, tie an uncooked fish (preferably mackerel) to the bottom of both feet and cover them with a sheet; keep in place overnight. In the morning, remove the fish and the fever will be gone.

☞ Soak a sheet in cold water and wrap yourself in it. Cover the wet sheet with a large beach towel or blanket; then lie down for about 15 minutes. Unwrap yourself when the wet sheet starts to get warm.

Nausea/Vomiting

☞ Mix one teaspoon of grated ginger with one teaspoon of juice from a raw onion, and then drink.

☞ Sip a cup of ginger tea.

☞ Drink some onion juice followed by a cup of cold peppermint tea.

☞ Drink cranberry juice.

☞ Drink a cup of tea mixed with a spoonful of honey and a squirt of fresh lemon juice.

☞ Mix one teaspoon of honey and one teaspoon lemon juice. Consume it slowly.

☞ Mix one cup of water with several drops of lime juice and half a teaspoon of sugar. Add a quarter of a teaspoon of baking soda, and drink.

☞ Crumble a lightly buttered piece of toast into one cup of warm milk. Consume it slowly.

OTHER INFECTIONS AND DISEASES

Warts

☞ Rub your warts with a piece of bacon that was stolen from a neighbour.

☞ Catch a frog and rub it on the wart.

☞ Soak a wart in water in which potatoes have been boiled.

☞ Touch the warts with a piece of string, tie a knot in the string for each wart and then bury the string in the ground.

☞ Spread butter on the wart and have a cat lick it clean.

☞ Wash the wart in water from the last snow of winter.

☞ Spit on the wart first thing every morning.

☞ Wash your hands outside under moonlight.

☞ Rub a piece of pork rind over it, wrap it in a piece of cloth and bury it in the ground.

☞ Or cut a potato in half and rub it on the wart. Throw the piece of potato over your shoulder, but don't look at it. When the potato rots, the wart will be gone.

☞ Rub a peeled apple over the wart, and give the apple to a pig.

☞ Cut notches in a stick for each wart you have, and then hide the stick.

☞ Rub a piece of fresh meat on any warts; then bury the meat. As it decays, the warts will disappear.

☞ Count the warts and make a like number of chalk marks on the back of a stove. As these burn off, the warts will go away.

☞ Soak a bean in water; then rub it on the wart. Plant the bean in the ground, and as it grows, the wart disappears.

☞ Wrap duct tape around the wart and leave it for several days; then remove.

☞ Circle the warts in horsehair.

☞ Soak a piece of cotton fabric in apple cider vinegar. Place it over the wart, and secure it in place. Do this every night, and remove during the day.

☞ Break a few leaves off of a milkweed plant and squeeze the bottom of the stem to release the sap. Apply enough sap to cover the wart. Leave on and reapply as needed.

☞ Twice a day, scrape the whitish mush off the inside of banana peel and apply it to your wart.

☞ Crush up about a quarter of a cup of fresh, well rinsed, basil leaves. Apply to the wart, cover with a bandage or clean cloth, and reapply daily until the wart is gone— about one to two weeks.

☞ Pull the head off of a dandelion and rub the milk onto the wart, and cover it with a bandage. Do this twice a day.

☞ File away the wart if you can; then cover it thoroughly in a thick layer of honey and wrap a piece of cloth around it. Leave it like this for 24 hours; then change the bandage and reapply the honey.

☞ Peel a potato and cut off a round slice. Rub the slice on your wart three times a day, and if you find yourself resting, lay the peeled skin over the wart for as long as possible.

☞ Soak your wart in pineapple juice for three to five minutes at least twice a day. Afterwards, pat the area completely dry.

☞ Ice the wart until the area is numb. Sterilize a sharp needle over a flame, then poke it well into the wart, but don't hold it there. Poke the wart all over. Discard the needle and wash your hands.

☞ Mix baking powder and castor oil into a paste; apply the paste to the wart at night, covering it with a bandage. Remove the bandage the next morning. Repeat as necessary.

☞ Dissolve baking soda in water; then wash your wart-plagued hand or foot in it. Let your hand dry naturally, with the baking soda still on it. Repeat often until the wart is gone.

☞ Rub crushed garlic or onion on your wart.

☞ Finely grate a carrot, and add enough olive oil to it to make a paste. Dab the paste on your wart twice daily, leaving it on for 30 minutes, for two to three weeks.

☞ Mash up a fresh fig and place some on your wart for 30 minutes. Do this once daily for two to three weeks.

☞ Squeeze a little lemon juice on your wart; then cover it with fresh, chopped onions for 30 minutes once a day for two to three weeks.

☞ After a rain storm, find an old tree stump where water has collected. Wash the warts in the stump water.

Boils

☞ Make a poultice of soap, flour and molasses on brown paper; then place it over the boil and secure it in place until the boil breaks and the infection is drained. For a stubborn boil, you may need to apply a new poultice throughout the day.

☞ To extract the core of a boil, put hot water in a glass bottle. Then empty the bottle and place its mouth over the boil. As the bottle cools, the core will come out.

☞ Make a poultice of raw potatoes; apply and change every eight hours.

☞ Heat one cup of milk and add three teaspoons of salt. Stir the mixture thoroughly. To make the mixture thick, add some bread crumbs or flour. Apply the thick mixture directly to the boil and cover with a clean cloth. Repeat the process several times in a day.

☞ Take some salt pork or bacon and roll it in salt. Place it between two pieces of cloth. Put the cloth directly on the boil. Repeat three times a day.

☞ Soak a small piece of the heel from a loaf of homemade white bread in boiling water—the older the bread, the better. Add a pinch of baking soda or salt. Squeeze any excess water from the bread. Lay the warm bread on sterile gauze or cloth and secure it over the boil. Keep in place for several hours.

Sties

☞ Mix equal parts of honey and warm milk. Keep stirring until the honey becomes smooth in the milk. Put two or three drops into your eyes several times a day, or use the mixture as a compress.

☞ Mix one tablespoon of apple cider vinegar with one cup of water. Soak a cotton ball and apply it to the sty.

☞ Soak a cotton ball in rose water, and place it over the eyes.

☛ Grate a potato, and place some of it on the sore eye. Grated potato may also be made into a poultice and placed over the eye for 15 minutes. Do this for three successive nights.

☛ Make an eyewash by mixing a quarter of a teaspoon of baking soda in a half cup of water. Submerge your eye completely in the solution, doing your best to hold it open. Roll it around for one full minute.

☛ Place cold bread on your eyelids; it will help reduce irritation, itchiness and inflammation.

☛ Make an eyewash by mixing a cup of distilled water with one teaspoon of salt. Boil the solution until the salt dissolves completely. Allow the solution to cool; then use it to flush the eyes. Repeat several times a day for two to three days.

☛ Soak fenugreek seeds in water for seven to eight hours; then make a smooth paste out of them. Apply the paste over your eyes and leave it on for 20 minutes. Wash the paste off with cold water. Do this twice daily for best results.

☛ The best home remedy for sore eyes is to gather the snow from a May snowfall. Once it melts, preserve the water in a sterile bottle and use as required.

☛ Make a solution using two teaspoons of goldenseal to one cup of boiled water and use for a warm compress. Also use as eye drops two or three times a day.

☛ Cut two slices of cucumber, place in ice water for 10 minutes and then place them on your closed eyelids for 10 minutes.

☛ Place four metal spoons in a glass of ice water. When chilled, place one spoon on each eye. As the spoons begin to warm, switch them with the spoons chilling in the ice water. Continue until swelling subsides.

☛ Use cotton balls soaked in witch-hazel extract as a compress over closed eyes.

☛ Put one drop of castor oil into each eye. Repeat this three times a day or as needed.

☛ Take a gold wedding band and rub it on the sty three times, each time rubbing in the same direction.

☛ Place a piece of uncooked pork or raw ground beef over the sty.

☛ Place a used, warm tea bag over the infected area. Do this several times a day.

☛ Massage the white from an egg onto the affected area.

Sore Mouth/Canker Sores/Cold Sores
☛ Rinsing your mouth with the dirty water from the blacksmith's forge will cure cold and canker sores.

☛ Rinse your mouth for several seconds with red wine. Repeat three times per day until mouth sores are gone.

☛ Rinse your mouth with goldenseal, red raspberry, white oak bark, wintergreen or witch-hazel extract.

☛ Add three teaspoons sage leaves to one pint of boiling water. Steep, covered, for 15 minutes. Rinse your mouth with the liquid several times a day.

☛ Crush dried sage leaves into a powder, and apply the powder directly to the sore area.

☛ Chew several jasmine leaves two or three times a day.

☛ Make a paste using baking soda and warm water, and apply to a canker sore.

☞ Rinse your mouth with a mixture of one teaspoon of baking soda, one teaspoon of salt and two ounces of hydrogen peroxide. Repeat four times daily.

☞ Rinse your mouth with lukewarm salt water and apply a little salt directly to the sore area.

☞ Put salt on a lemon slice and hold it on the sore for about 10 minutes.

☞ Coat your mouth with honey mixed with lemon juice. Then swish around some salt water; spit. Then swish around some buttermilk.

☞ Mix cayenne pepper in a glass of water and rinse your mouth with the mixture. If you have a cold sore, dab the mixture on the affected area.

☞ Apply garlic oil to the affected area.

☞ Rub aftershave on a cold sore.

Chicken Pox

☛ Boil several cups of fresh green peas. Drain, but keep the water. Crush the peas into a paste, and apply the paste to the affected area. Allow it dry for about one hour before washing it off using the water in which the peas were cooked.

☛ Add two cups of Epsom salts to your warm bathwater, and soak for about 15 minutes.

Shingles

☛ Apply apple cider vinegar four times during the day and three times during the night if you are awake.

☛ Make a lotion by mixing cold tea, a drop of honey, a drop of lemon juice and a drop of vinegar, and apply to the affected areas.

☛ They say that one of the best ways to treat shingles is to rub on fresh blood from a cat's tail. However, they don't say how you should get that blood.

Ringworm

☛ Circle it with your wedding ring; then cross it three times.

☛ Make a paste by mixing shortening with cigarette or pipe ash, and apply it to the affected area.

☛ Apply apple cider vinegar or white vinegar directly to the affected area and leave on for at least 10 minutes before washing.

☛ Make a paste using baking soda and hydrogen peroxide. Apply it to the affected area.

☛ Rub the oil from a green walnut shell over the affected area.

☛ Rub the oil from the dipstick of your car over the affected area and leave on until it wears off. Repeat as often as necessary until the infection is cleared up.

Foot Fungus
☛ If you urinate on your feet when you are in the shower, the fungus will go away. Do this once a day for a week.

COSMETIC COMPLAINTS

Black Eye

☛ Peel and cut a potato into thick slices. Put the potato slices in the refrigerator for half an hour. Then place a cold potato slice over the affected eye for half an hour. Or grate a potato to squeeze out the juice, and apply the juice to the blackened eye.

☛ Soak a cloth in witch-hazel extract, and place it on the affected eye for a few minutes.

☛ Massage the affected area with olive oil or castor oil.

☛ Dip a tea bag in water; then place it in the freezer. Once the tea bag has frozen, place it on the black eye.

Chapped Lips

☛ Mix one teaspoon of castor oil, one teaspoon of sugar and a few drops of fresh lemon juice. Apply to your lips before going to bed. In the morning, wash it off with lukewarm water. Repeat daily until your lips are healed.

☛ Apply fresh milk cream to your lips and leave it on for 10 minutes. Then gently wash your lips with lukewarm water. Repeat daily until your lips are healed.

☛ Rub honey on your sore lips before going to bed.

☛ Massage cracked lips with a dab of earwax (preferably your own).

Cracked Hands

☞ Wash and dry your hands thoroughly, then apply vinegar. Put on a pair of soft gloves and leave them on overnight.

☞ Make a cornmeal paste by combining a quarter of a cup of cornmeal with one teaspoon of water and a drop of apple cider vinegar. Rub the paste over your dry hands and allow it to dry for 10 to 15 minutes; then rinse them with warm water.

Ingrown Nails
☞ Drop hot tallow from a lit candle onto the sore part of the nail and leave in place to soften the nail.

Pimples/Acne
☞ Apply whipped egg whites to your face and let sit for several minutes. Wash off with warm water.

☞ Wash your face with water, and leave it a bit damp. Grate one raw potato, and rub the pulp and juice onto your face. Let it dry for about 30 minutes; then rinse with warm water.

☞ Mix honey and mashed up strawberries together. Apply the mixture to your face and let it sit for 20 minutes. Rinse off with warm water. Repeat every day for a week.

Baldness

☞ Beat an egg yolk with some honey until the texture is smooth and creamy. Apply it on the bald patches and allow to set for 30 minutes. Rinse off with cool water.

☞ Mix the white of one egg with a teaspoon of olive oil. Beat to give a paste-like consistency, and apply the mixture to your scalp. Keep it on for 15 to 20 minutes; then rinse with cool water.

☛ Mix a tablespoon of honey in a glass of brandy. Add a few drops of onion juice; then massage the mixture on your head. Wrap your head and leave it overnight. The next morning, rinse it clean with warm water.

☛ Make a paste by crushing garlic and adding honey. Massage the mixture into your scalp.

☛ Finely chop an onion and squeeze out the juice. Apply to the scalp and leave on for about 15 minutes; then rinse with water. Next, crush a few cloves of garlic, add in a little coconut oil and boil for a few minutes. When this mixture cools down to feel warm to the touch, massage it into the scalp. Repeat two to three times a week.

☛ Mix lemon juice and gooseberry juice in equal proportions. Apply it to the bald patches.

☛ Cut a few gooseberries into pieces, and dry them in the shade. Boil some coconut oil and add the dried gooseberries. Boil until the hard parts are cooked and turn dark. Gently massage your scalp with this oil.

☛ Boil geranium leaves in water for 10 minutes. Apply the cooled solution to the bald patches.

☛ Boil a cup of mustard oil with the remains of tobacco from a pipe. Let it cool down and then gently massage it on the affected areas. Leave on for several hours.

☛ Rub cow manure on your head once a day for an entire week to encourage your hair to grow.

Dandruff

☛ Mix two teaspoons of vinegar in a cup of beet juice. Massage the mixture into your scalp and let it sit for about an hour, then rinse. Repeat daily until the dandruff clears up.

☛ Wash your hair and scalp in tea.

OUTDOOR DANGERS

Poison Ivy

☛ Pat a small amount of witch-hazel extract directly on the affected skin.

☛ Apply strongly brewed tea to the affected area and let it dry. Repeat as needed.

☛ Mix a small amount of powdered goldenseal root with a small amount of hot water. Rub the paste on the affected skin.

☛ Place slices of fresh cucumber on the affected area, or mash them up to make a cucumber paste before applying to the affected skin.

☛ Mix baking soda and water; rub the mixture on the affected area.

☛ Mix equal parts of apple cider vinegar and water. Dab on the affected skin areas and allow to dry.

☛ Soak a brown paper bag in apple cider vinegar, and place it on the rash.

☛ Rub the inside of a banana peel on poison ivy-affected skin.

☛ Rub watermelon rinds on the rash.

☛ Grind one cup of oatmeal into a fine powder, then pour it into a piece of cheesecloth. Knot the material into a pouch and hang it on the faucet of your bathtub so the bag is suspended under the running water. Fill the tub with lukewarm water, and soak in it for 30 minutes. Or make an oatmeal pouch as described above, but apply it directly to the rash.

Insect Stings and Bites

☛ Rub plantain leaves, known locally as pigs ears, until moist, and apply to the sting.

☛ Pack red dirt on the sting and hold it in place until the pain subsides. It is said to draw the poison from the sting area. When I was growing up, we would pack it on the painful sting for a minute or so, and then replace it with a fresh packing of soil. It was quite effective.

☛ Rub a slice of onion over an insect bite to stop the itching and help prevent infection.

Splinters

☛ Place a slice of raw potato on the splinter such that the fleshy part touches the splinter, and press the potato slice downwards. If the sliver pierces the slice, it can be lifted out easily.

Sunburns

☛ Simply apply a cold cloth or a few ice cubes wrapped in a towel directly to the burn.

☛ Wrap half a cup of dry oatmeal in gauze, run it under cool water, and apply it directly to your sunburn every few hours.

☛ Use yogurt as a topical cream and slather it over sunburned areas, leaving it for five to 10 minutes, then rinse off using cool water.

☛ If your eyelids are burned, apply used tea bags to each lid for quick relief.

☛ Apply vinegar to the areas that are burned.

☛ Mix raw eggs in warm water; apply the mixture to affected areas.

☛ Apply a few drops of witch-hazel extract to a moist cloth, and dab it onto your skin.

- Put a bit of baking soda in a lukewarm bath and soak in the water for at least 15 minutes. When you get out, allow your skin to air dry. Do not use a towel.

- Add a cup of apple cider vinegar to your bath water, or apply it directly to the burn.

- Bathe in milk.

RANDOM CURES FOR RANDOM MALADIES

Personal Protection

☛ If you hang a piece of clothing from a sick person in a tree, the patient will recover.

☛ Sealing hair clippings in bored holes in the front door will prevent asthma from inflicting the person whose hair is in the door.

Animal Therapy

☛ A country cure for thrush was to hold a live frog to the patient's mouth. As the frog breathed in, it was supposed to draw out the disease into its own body.

☛ Inhaling a horse's breath is said to cure whooping cough.

Swallow Your Medicine

☛ Drink black coffee to sober up if you have been drinking.

☛ To cure a hangover, mix tomato juice and beer in a tall glass and drink.

☛ If your child is wetting the bed, give him or her one teaspoon of the pulp of Indian gooseberry mixed with a pinch of black pepper before going to bed.

DID YOU KNOW?

It is said that children who play in an open fire will wet their beds.

Feathers, Fur and Creepy Crawlies

Throughout the generations, civilizations have observed the behaviour of birds, bugs and other animals for clues about the world around them. This is especially true in Atlantic Canada, where we find many superstitions with animals big and small at their core.

FEATHERS

Supernatural Crows

There is a common saying in Atlantic Canada that goes:

One crow sorrow, two crows joy;
Three crows a girl, four crows a boy;
Five crows silver, six crows gold;
Seven crows a secret yet to be told;
Eight crows a wish, nine crows a kiss;
Ten crows a time of joyous bliss.

Depending upon the region of Atlantic Canada in which one is raised, this traditional verse has variations such as:

Seeing a single crow is very unlucky.
Two crows mean good luck!
Three mean health.
Four mean wealth.
Five is sickness.
Six mean death!

and

One crow for sorrow, two crows for mirth;
Three crows for a wedding, four crows for a birth;
Five crows for silver, six crows for gold;
Seven crows for a secret, not to be told;
Eight crows for heaven, nine crows for hell;
And ten crows for the Devil's own self.

Luckily, there are ways to protect yourself if you do see one crow.

- ☞ If you see a single crow, you can blow it a kiss to prevent the sorrow. Other ways to fend off the bad luck associated with seeing one crow are to spit, or to make the sign of the cross and raise your hat to the bird.

- ☞ A spell of protection against the power of one crow was to spit three times over your right shoulder and say, "Devil, Devil, I defy thee."

DID YOU KNOW?

When you are thinking of something bad or if you have worries, you should spit over your left shoulder, and things will get better.

Beyond these traditional rhymes are many beliefs focusing on the reputed supernatural power of crows.

- First Nations people believed that crows were sent to Earth to escort the souls of the recently deceased to meet their creator.

- A single crow in a cemetery is said to be a sign that there will be a funeral within the week.

- It's believed that the visit and call of the crow is an omen of impending death. Another version suggests that a single crow flying over a house means bad news, and often foretells a death within. There is an old saying that goes: *A crow over the thatch, soon death lifts the latch.* However, if a crow perches on a house, it was said to bring prosperity to the family within.

- If a crow sits on your wash line in the morning, someone in the family will die that day.

- Two crows flying over a house means that there will soon be a birth in that household.

- Seeing two crows flying together from the left is said to be bad luck.

- It is bad luck to see a single crow at a wedding, but good luck to see a pair of crows as it means years of continuous happiness will follow the bride and groom. Often, in fact, in earlier times, two crows would be released together during a wedding celebration. If the two birds flew away together, the couple could look forward to a long life together. However, if the pair separated, the couple might expect to be parted soon, too. (This practice was also performed using pairs of doves.)

- To hear three crows cawing is said to be bad luck.

☛ Finding a dead crow on the road is good luck.

☛ It is unlucky to have a crow cross your path. However, if two crows cross your path, the luck is reversed, as in this saying: *Two crows I see, good luck to me.*

☛ Crows feeding in the streets or close to nests in the morning means inclement weather is coming—usually storms or rain. Conversely, crows flying far from their nest is a sign that fair weather is approaching.

If crows fly low, wind's going to blow;
If crows fly high, wind's going to die.

☛ It was once believed that when crows were quiet and subdued during their midsummer's moult, they were preparing to go to the Devil to pay tribute with their black feathers.

☛ In some places, crows were thought to be so evil that it was believed each one had a drop of the Devil's blood under its tongue.

☛ To break the curse of the crows, you could carry an onion for protection.

Other Birds

☛ Dreaming of birds, particularly crows or owls, means you will soon receive some bad news. But if those birds are doves or sparrows, the news will be good.

☛ You know spring has arrived when you see your first robin. If you make a wish on the first robin you see in spring, it will come true.

- It is said that happiness and good fortune will follow if you see an albino (white) robin or blue jay.

- If a robin enters your house, it's a sign of a death in the family.

- It is bad luck to kill a sparrow because they are said to carry the souls of the dead.

- It is good luck for swallows to build their nests in your home because they protect it from fire and also bring prosperity to all within. If you destroy a nest, someone in the home will soon die.

- An owl perched on your house is a sign of death.

- It is bad luck to see an owl in the daylight.

- If you hear a woodpecker, you will soon be coming into money.

- If three seagulls fly together, directly overhead, it's a warning that death will come soon.

When sea birds fly to land,
there truly is a storm at hand.

FUR

Mice

☛ If a mouse is discovered in the house, it's thought that someone in that house will soon die. In another version of this belief, a mouse in the house can also foretell a terrible tragedy such as an accident or fire. In still another version, it means someone is thinking bad thoughts about someone who lives there and may wish them harm.

☛ If a cat brings a mouse to your house, it means no one in your home will go hungry.

☛ You should allow your cat to kill as many mice as it can because with every mouse it kills, it also kills one of your enemies.

☛ It is bad luck to bury a dead mouse in your yard; if you do, nothing will ever grow there again.

Cats

☛ If a cat sleeps on its brain (upside down), it's going to rain. Or, if a cat sits with its back towards a fire, it will rain. And if a cat licks its tail, it's yet another sign of rain.

☛ Good luck will come to your household if you own a three-coloured cat.

☞ If you are moving into a brand new house that has not yet been lived in, it is good luck to first let a cat walk through the door before you cross the threshold. It is also suggested that whichever bedroom the cat first lies down in, that is where you should put your bed.

☞ Dreaming of cats is usually a sign that something evil has entered your life, but if you dream about a white cat, good luck will follow.

☞ It is bad luck for a cat to jump onto a table.

☞ If you encounter a cat when you leave your house in the morning, it's a sign of bad luck to come.

☞ It is especially bad luck if a black cat crosses your path. A black cat crossing your path by moonlight means death is coming. Our modern-day fear of black cats may stem from the Middle Ages, when it was believed that a witch could take the form of a black cat. If you see a black cat, you should either spit three times over your left shoulder or take seven steps backward in order to get your luck back. Ironically, in England, a black cat crossing your path is said to be lucky.

☞ If a stray black cat takes up its home at a house, the unmarried daughters will have a good chance to marry.

Dogs

☞ It was once believed that if a dog howled for no obvious reason, something tragic was about to happen.

☞ If a dog sleeps facing north, it means there's a bad winter storm coming.

☞ If a dog breaks wind, it's a sign that a bad storm is coming.

☛ If a dog buries its bone in your garden, it means a poor harvest that year.

☛ If a dog barks at the door of your home, but there is no one there, it means the spirit of someone recently deceased has visited your house.

☛ It is bad luck for a dog to run between a woman's legs.

☛ Many consider it a good omen if a dog eats grass.

☛ If a dog chases its tail, it means a ship will sink.

DID YOU  KNOW?

If you receive an animal such as a dog or a cat as a gift, you should give a coin in return as token payment. If not, you will have bad luck as long as that animal is alive.

Horses

☛ Changing a horse's name is said to be bad luck.

☛ Grey horses and horses with four white feet are considered unlucky. However, if a bride and groom see a grey horse on the way to the church, it is considered lucky.

☛ If you break a mirror, the misfortune can be averted if you lead a horse through the house. The same applies if you spill salt in the kitchen.

☛ If you lead a white horse through your house, it will banish all evil.

☛ Dreaming of horses usually means that someone is on their way to visit. But dreaming of a white horse is considered a death omen.

☛ If you walk under a ladder it is considered bad luck, but you can avoid the bad luck if you keep your fingers crossed until you have seen three horses.

☛ Horses and witches don't mix. If you wear a hair from the tail of a black stallion on your wrist, you will be protected from witches. The tail of a horse is adorned with ribbons not for beauty but to keep the animal safe from witches. And horse brasses are used to protect horses from witches because brass is a metal that witches fear.

CREEPY CRAWLIES

The Buzz About Bees

☛ A beekeeper should talk to his bees every day and keep them up to date on everything happening in his personal life. If he neglects to tell his bees of an engagement, birth or death in the family, he risks the entire swarm deserting their hive.

☛ You should try to resist the urge to swat a bee landing on your hand because the tiny winged wonder is trying to tell you that wealth and good fortune reside in your future. If you do kill the bee, then that good luck will turn to bad.

☛ If a bee enters your house, it is a sign that you will soon have a visitor. If you kill the bee, either you will have bad luck or the visitor will be unpleasant.

☛ A swarm of bees settling on a roof is an omen that the house will soon burn down.

Fluttery Folklore

☛ If the first butterfly you see in the spring is white, it means you will have good luck for the remainder of the year.

☛ It is good luck to see three butterflies in flight together.

☛ It is considered a sign of good luck if a butterfly flutters around your head.

☛ If you see a luna moth, you will eventually go mad.

☛ A white moth inside the house or trying to enter the house is said to mean death for someone inside the house.

☛ To see a butterfly at night is to see death approaching.

My Lucky Bug

☛ It is considered good luck if a ladybug lands on you; it means you will have a long, healthy life. Discovering a ladybug in your home is also said to be good luck. It is bad luck to kill any ladybug because they symbolize the Virgin Mary.

☛ Finding a grasshopper in your house is good luck. If a grasshopper jumps on you, good fortune will follow.

☛ If a cricket manages to get into your house and starts to chirp, it's considered good luck. It is bad luck to kill a cricket.

☛ It is rare to find a praying mantis, so if a woman finds one, it is considered to be very good luck. If a man finds a praying mantis, it's a sign of his virility and that he can father lots of children.

☛ Ants are believed to be carriers of good news, and as such, you should not kill them, even if they are inside your house. If you leave them be, they will bring good luck.

Insect Weather

☞ To hear crickets sing in the morning before sunrise is a sign of a stormy day. Hearing crickets sing at night means clear weather ahead.

☞ If hornets build their nests close to the ground, it means an open winter with little snow.

☞ Finding a mosquito in your house in winter is a sign the coming summer will be wet.

Spiders

A spider in the morning is a sign of sorrow;
A spider at noon brings worry for tomorrow;
A spider in the afternoon is a sign of a gift;
But a spider in the evening will all hopes uplift.

☞ If spiders build their webs high off the ground in the summer and fall, it means lots of snow in the winter.

☞ If you find a spider in your house in January, it means you should expect an early spring.

☞ If you kill a spider, it will rain.

☞ Finding a spider in a drinking glass is said to be bad luck and can also mean that you will soon be sick.

☞ Finding a spider in your kitchen sink is a sign that a tragedy is about to befall your household.

☞ If you find a spider on your neck, it means that you have a secret admirer.

- If you find a spider in your bed, it means that your marriage is in trouble.

- If a spider spins its web outside a window, then someone who lives within is about to be caught in a lie.

- To see a spider spinning its web in the morning is lucky.

- Seeing a spider run down its web in the middle of the afternoon means you are going to take a trip.

- If you find a spider in your shoe, it means you are going to be taking a long trip.

DID YOU  KNOW?

It is a widely held belief in Atlantic Canada that when someone leaves the house to go on a trip, the one who is left behind must throw some water, for instance a cup full, out the door in the direction the traveller took. Doing this will mean good luck will follow the traveller, just as water flows freely down a river.

Snakes

- If you kill the first snake you see in the spring, it is said you kill your worst enemy.

- Finding a snake in your house is said to be bad luck.

Wood Ticks

These beliefs about wood ticks are all myths, but try telling that to an Atlantic Canadian.

- Once attached to the body, ticks should never be pulled off because if their head or legs break off under the skin, the area will become infected and poison your body.

☛ Heat is the only effective method to make a tick detach from the body.

☛ The only way to kill a wood tick is to burn it.

☛ Wood ticks are so tough they cannot be crushed.

☛ Ticks can jump from one host to the next.

BUG OFF

What do you do when the little pests won't leave you alone? Well, depending where you find yourself in Atlantic Canada, you would encounter various suggestions about how to protect yourself from those creatures that like to dine on you.

Plant Repellents

☛ Plant marigolds in your gardens. Insects, especially mosquitoes, are said to hate the flowers' scent. Try planting them throughout your vegetable garden, or place pots of them on your deck and patio.

☛ Sage, rosemary, lavender and mint are also said to be effective, natural bug repellents. Try keeping a few pots of these herbs around your outdoor spaces.

Food Repellents

☛ Slices of cucumber spread around your picnic blanket will keep the ants from invading.

☛ Garlic is good for keeping away flies, mosquitoes and ants. Place it around your yard and house if you can tolerate the smell. And eating garlic is said to be a good way to keep the mosquitoes from biting.

☛ Lemon juice and cinnamon are also worth a try. Try spreading the mixture around your deck or wherever you're going to be.

☛ Orange peelings are supposedly good at repelling mosquitoes.

Dress to Repel

☛ The clothes you wear may attract the little pests. Wearing light coloured clothing is supposed to keep the mosquitoes from bothering you.

☛ Also, people who wear hats or keep their heads covered are said to be bothered less by mosquitoes than those who do not.

☛ Smear yourself with baby oil to keep the mosquitoes from biting.

Smoke Them Out

☛ Smoke will keep mosquitoes at bay, particularly if it's wood smoke from burning maple.

☛ Burning dried cow manure will keep the flies away.

Protect Your Plants

☛ A mixture of soap and water is good for keeping earwigs under control as well as other pests that enjoy munching on your plants.

☛ Spread crushed eggshells throughout your garden to keep away slugs and snails.

☛ Place small containers of beer throughout your gardens to keep slugs from eating your plants. They'll drown in the beer instead.

Indoor Pests

☛ Baking soda is good for killing pet odours and other smells.

☛ If you have fleas in your carpets, sprinkle sea salt around your floors and then quickly vacuum.

☛ It was said that drizzling honey around a room on Sunday would drive out evil forces and would also kill all the pests that might nest there.

How's Your Green Thumb?

In Atlantic Canada, there are many superstitions that grow from gardening and gardeners.

FLOWER FOLKLORE

Gardens in Bloom

☛ Flowers planted during the new moon will bloom best.

☛ Sunflowers bring good luck to the entire garden.

☛ Flowers that bloom out of season, such as crocuses, which normally bloom in the spring, are a sign of a harsh winter.

Get Well Soon

☛ Snowdrops are beautiful little white flowers that bloom in the late winter. They are said to be a symbol of purity and hope. However, if they are taken inside a house where there is a sick person, they are said be an omen of death.

☛ It is unlucky for a sick person to place flowers on their bed.

When you are giving flowers to someone who is ill, you should remember the superstitions attached to flower colours:

☞ White flowers are bad luck for any sick person. Red, however, denotes blood and life and is good luck.

☞ Never give a bunch of red and white mixed together, especially to a hospital patient.

☞ Violet shows goodwill on the part of the giver.

☞ Yellow and orange are the colour of the sun and will please anyone whatever their state of health.

Flower of the Month

According to the month of your birth, these are your lucky flowers:

☞ January: carnations and snowdrops
☞ February: primroses
☞ March: daffodils
☞ April: daisies
☞ May: lilies of the valley
☞ June: roses
☞ July: water lilies
☞ August: gladioli
☞ September: asters
☞ October: dahlias
☞ November: chrysanthemums
☞ December: holly

IN THE VEGETABLE PATCH

Rules to Grow By

☞ Some gardeners swear by planting their potatoes or root crops in the dark or waning of the moon. Others always plant potatoes during the full moon to ensure a healthy harvest.

☞ Peas, beans, corn... all those vegetables that grow in the sun, plant in the full or growing moon.

☞ If you plant your beans before 9:00 AM, you will be assured a healthy crop.

☞ Always plant cucumber seeds just before dawn.

☞ Never plant before the last frost in June.

☞ Never thank the person who gives you plants or seeds because if you do, the plants and seeds will not grow.

☞ Pouring a mixture of milk and honey in a hole in your garden soil will keep your garden healthy.

☞ Putting rusty nails in your garden will make the plants grow better.

☞ Rotting seaweed makes good fertilizer.

Pesky Kitty

If cats are a nuisance in your garden, Atlantic Canadians have several homegrown methods of keeping them out.

☞ Spread orange or lemon peelings throughout your garden to keep stray cats from turning it into a litter box.

However, these will have to be replenished every couple of days as they dry out.

☛ Pepper is a deterrent. Black pepper may work, but some say that chili or cayenne pepper works better. Some people also say cats don't like garlic either.

☛ Mouthwash, molasses, detergent and beer are all said to be good for keeping the cats away when poured over the soil.

☛ Pipe tobacco may work. Chewing tobacco has also been suggested.

☛ Some people suggest that spreading coffee grounds over the ground will stop the cats from digging.

☛ Sprinkling broken eggshells throughout your garden will keep the cats out and makes great fertilizer.

☛ Spread mothballs around the perimeter of the garden.

☛ Place pieces of aluminum foil around your garden.

☛ Try sticking plastic forks around your garden, but they have to be close enough so the cat can't get between them.

☞ Pinecones are said to act as a deterrent to digging.

☞ Spread human hair around your garden; cats will avoid it.

☞ Try planting geraniums, marigolds and petunias. Cats apparently don't like their scent.

☞ If you plant spiky plants throughout your garden, the cats will stay out.

☞ Placing mulch around the borders of your garden may work.

☞ Get your own cat. It will not poop in its own yard, and other cats will not invade its territory.

☞ Or, as a last resort, you could pee in your own garden. The human scent will keep the cats away.

THE GRASS IS ALWAYS GREENER

Magic Mushrooms

☛ Large circles of mushrooms, known as fairy rings, were once believed to be the work of magic. Many people thought misfortune—perhaps serious illness or even death—awaited anyone foolhardy enough to enter into the middle of such a natural phenomenon.

☛ A house built in a field where fairy rings have grown is said to be filled with happiness.

DID YOU KNOW?

It was thought to be good luck if you burned mushrooms, but not so good if you allowed your cattle to graze in a pasture where mushrooms grow.

Making a Living

Folks in Atlantic Canada have traditionally made their living by toiling on the land or by fishing on the ocean.

ON THE FARM

Like other rural regions, people throughout Atlantic Canada also have many superstitions when it comes to farming and farm animals.

In the Farmyard

☛ It is good luck to have a cat on your farm, to say nothing about keeping the mouse population under control.

☛ It is said that on a farm, a whistling girl and a crowing rooster will surely come to a bad end.

Cattle Chatter

☛ It is believed that cattle talk on Christmas Eve, and if you hear them, you will die.

☛ If cattle are observed lying down in the pasture, it is a sign that rain is on the way.

☛ Farmers believe that if the spring's first calf is breach, it's a bad omen for the rest of the year.

☛ If a calf is stillborn, someone on the farm will soon die.

☛ If a white calf is born in winter, you should prepare for harsh weather.

☛ If a cow is milked outside the barn while it is standing on the ground, the animal will dry up.

☛ If you sing inside the barn, the cows will not give milk.

☛ If a cow doesn't give milk for a week, it's a sign of a harsh winter.

☞ Feeding honey to cows is said to keep them healthy. Rubbing honey in the eyes of a sick cow will make it get better.

Horseplay

☞ If horses are standing close together in the pasture, you should expect rain.

☞ If a horse stands with its back to the barn door, it's going to rain.

☞ If a horse neighs at the door of a house, it is a sign of sickness for the inhabitants.

Don't Be Chicken

☞ If the hens don't lay eggs for three consecutive days, it's a sign that a tragedy is about to befall the farm.

☞ If hens lay their eggs outside the henhouse, it's a sign that fair weather is coming.

☞ If the hens nest in the morning, it's a sign of impending death, usually that of the farmer or someone in the family.

☞ If a hen or a rooster gets inside the farmhouse, it means there is going to be a visitor that day.

☞ It is bad luck to hear a rooster crowing at night. If a rooster crows three times between sunset and midnight, it's a sign that a death will soon occur.

☞ If a rooster crows close to the door of your house, someone is going to die.

DID YOU KNOW?

When it comes to slaughtering chickens, many people in Atlantic Canada believe it should be left to a man. A woman should not do it or even be present; otherwise, bad luck and misfortune will befall the household.

Out in the Fields

☞ It is bad luck to plough the fields on Sunday.

☞ If it starts to rain while ploughing, it's a sign of a good crop to come.

☞ Crops that are planted on the 31st of any month will not grow.

☞ Some farmers believe that if they take a fresh egg into the fields in spring, the result will be a healthy crop. Cracking a fresh egg in the fields in fall will protect the crop from frost.

☞ Blessing a field with honey will also produce a healthy crop.

Orchard Offerings

☛ If, on the first day of spring, you burn scraps of food around the base of fruit trees, they will be more fruitful.

☛ If the sun shines through the apple trees on Christmas or Easter, the fruit will be plentiful in the next harvest.

☛ Apple growers believe it is good luck to eat the first apple of the fall harvest because it assures them good prices at market.

☛ It is good luck to plant an apple core in your orchard because it will fertilize your entire crop.

DOWN UNDERGROUND

Mining is one of the most dangerous professions in which to earn a living, and Atlantic Canada has been devastated by one mining disaster after another. Along with the tragedies comes a list of superstitions that have evolved from the industry.

Reading the Signs

Miners always lit candles down in the mine because the flame would go out if insufficient oxygen was in the air, signalling them to get out. Superstitious miners believed that if they saw rats scampering to get out of the mine, they should also make for the exits because it was a sign that there would be a cave in.

Avoiding Bad Luck

☞ If, on the way to the mine, a miner realizes he forgot something at home, he should leave it there and continue on to work. It is bad luck to go back and fetch it.

☞ Miners believe that if a cat or dog crosses their path while they are heading for the mine, then something bad is going to happen that day.

☞ It is bad luck for a miner to see a pig while on his way to work. If he does, he should miss his shift to avoid disaster. It is also bad luck to utter the word "pig" down in the mine, as it will cause a cave in.

☞ It is thought to be bad luck for a woman to enter a mine.

ON THE SEA

Over the centuries, sailors and fishermen have created hundreds of customs to govern their behaviour at sea. Most are quirky; some are flat-out bizarre. As would be expected from people who reside in Atlantic Canada, there are many superstitions in the region stemming from the sea. But regardless of origin, all served a similar purpose: to help ensure the safety of the sailors on the wild, unpredictable ocean.

No Girls Allowed

Women were viewed as being unlucky at sea. Apparently the presence of a woman on board could stir up bad weather. A naked woman, however, was another matter. A bare-breasted woman had the power to calm the sea, thus explaining the presence of a female-shaped figurehead on the bow of many ships.

☞ In some Maritime communities, it is considered bad luck to take a woman fishing because she will keep the fish from biting.

☞ Some people also believe it is bad luck to have anyone with red hair on board.

Fair Weather

On the water, you must not do anything to jinx the weather. Whistling during a fair breeze is seen as a sure way to bring on a strong, contrary wind or even a storm. Only two people can whistle on a ship: the captain because he knows how to control the wind, and the cook because it is impossible to whistle while you're chewing. And if the cook is whistling, then he isn't eating.

☞ You must never bring an umbrella on deck; it suggests that there will be a rainstorm.

☞ Throwing rocks in the ocean will bring on a storm.

☞ It is bad luck to stick a knife in the mast because it will bring on a big wind.

Banana Ban

A fear of bananas on board was more logical in its origin—crates of bananas could hold poisonous spiders and snakes. The fruit was also known to release deadly methane gas into the hold, suffocating anyone trapped inside. Ripening bananas also cause other fruit to ripen faster; on a long voyage, the entire food supply could spoil, causing sailors to go hungry. And, of course, a slippery peel could end up under the foot of a sailor.

☞ Some fishermen believe that having bananas on board means they will not catch any fish.

Animals at Sea

Animals were often central to seafaring superstitions. For example, a shark following a ship indicated that someone would soon die; cats (though welcomed on board) were believed to house lightning bolts and storms in their tail.

And the killing of an albatross was considered a major offence—an albatross, it was believed, carried the soul of a dead sailor.

☛ Dogs on board a ship are bad luck, but black cats on board are actually considered a sign of good luck.

☛ Dolphins swimming near a ship are believed to be good luck.

☛ It is bad luck to say the word "pig" on board a ship. Pigs have cloven hoofs, which supposedly reminds people of the Devil. It is also bad luck to say "rabbit," though no one knows why.

☛ Seeing a swallow at sea is good luck, but seeing a cormorant is bad luck.

☛ It is unlucky to kill a gull because, like albatrosses, gulls are said to possess the souls of dead sailors.

☛ Every time a sea gull cries, a fisherman dies somewhere in the world.

☛ If a crow flies over the left side of a boat, something bad will happen. If it flies past on the right side, the boat's crew is safe.

Maiden Voyage Musts

Many age-old customs continue today, like dousing a new boat with liquor. In ancient times, the Greeks poured red wine onto the deck of a new ship, as well as into the sea, as part of a sacrifice to the ocean gods. Red wine, chosen for its blood-like appearance, was later replaced with Champagne—a more expensive sacrifice.

☛ It is a sign that a ship will be plagued with tragedy if the bottle does not smash during its launching.

☛ It is bad luck to change the name of a vessel once it's been christened.

☛ It is bad luck to have 13 characters in the name of a ship.

☛ It is good luck to have A's in the name of a ship, especially three of them.

☛ Do not use blue paint on any boat, but particularly a lobster boat.

Bon Voyage

☛ It is bad luck to have a total of 13 members in a ship's crew.

☛ It is bad luck to launch a boat or leave port on a Friday. Most ships would depart no later than 11:59 PM on Thursday and no earlier than 12:01 AM on Saturday.

☛ It is also thought to be bad luck to start a trip on the first Monday in April, the second Monday in August and on December 31.

☛ It is good luck to leave on a Sunday.

☛ It is bad luck to wish good luck to someone heading out to sea.

☛ It is bad luck to step onto a boat with your left foot first.

☛ Always turn starboard first after backing away from the dock.

☛ It is bad luck to look back once the ship has left port.

DID YOU KNOW?

If you dream of running water, it means you are going to take a trip on a boat.

Seafaring Etiquette

☞ Cutting your hair or fingernails at sea is bad luck.

☞ Spitting into the ocean can break a spell of bad luck.

☞ It is bad luck to pee over the side of a ship. However, having a virgin pee on a new net before it is brought on board is said to be good luck and will lead to bigger catches.

☞ It is bad luck to say "drowned" while you're at sea.

☞ Never speak of the Devil while at sea, or tragedy will strike.

☞ If you could skip a rock through the crest of a wave, you would be able to cut the Devil's throat.

☞ Losing a mop or bucket overboard is bad luck.

☞ When going aloft, it is bad luck to pass through the shrouds leading to the ratlines. One must always go around the shrouds, fore or aft, but never through them.

☞ It is bad luck to leave a hatch upside down because it could result in the ship being turned over.

☞ It is bad luck to turn anything—cups, glasses or bowls— upside down on board a ship. Such action is said to bring on a powerful wave that will cause the vessel to capsize. You're not even to open a can upside down. It's so bad that I won't even do that when I'm on land.

☞ Do not coil a rope or stir a pot counter clockwise.

☞ Having flowers, coffins or priests on board were all seen as ill-fated because of their connection to funerals. And if you meet a minister just before setting sail, bad luck is sure to accompany the voyage.

☞ Hearing church bells while you're at sea means someone on the ship will soon die.

☛ Never ring a bell unnecessarily on board a ship because it means a sailor somewhere it going to die. On most ships, the bell is kept wrapped in cloth and the clapper is kept secured. They only ring the bell when the occasion calls for it.

DID YOU KNOW?

When a fisherman is lost overboard, it is customary to place a lit candle on a slice of bread and set it adrift. This, it is said, will comfort the lost crewman.

Drink to Your Health

☛ Whenever any alcoholic beverage is served on board a ship, before anyone takes a drink, you must offer a drink to Neptune and offer a drink to the ship's deck.

☛ Ringing the rim of an empty wineglass is believed to guarantee the death of one sailor by drowning.

☛ Others believe that when the rim of a glass rings, it's a sign that there will be a shipwreck.

Watch What You Wear

☛ It is said that if the clothes of a dead sailor are worn by another sailor during the same voyage, tragedy will strike onboard.

☛ Some fishermen believe it is bad luck to wear black on a boat because black is the colour of death.

☛ Other colours to avoid are green—it makes the boat seek land—and yellow—because of its association with bananas.

☞ Mittens worn on a ship always had to be white. Grey especially was not allowed because grey mittens brought grey skies. Having someone on board with mittens that were not white could send a captain back to shore to begin a voyage again—that is, after the coloured mittens were disposed of.

☞ Sailors once wore large gold earrings in the left ear so they would have money safely attached to their body to pay the ferryman for the trip into the next world in case they drowned.

☞ It is bad luck to wear a hat in the galley.

Driving the Whisky Plank

Sea-faring communities in much of Atlantic Canada where ships are built have adopted a special tradition believed to bring good luck and good fortune to their vessels. The last plank laid during the construction of a ship's hull is commonly referred to as the Whisky Plank. The practice of making an occasion out of laying the whisky plank is a long-standing wooden shipbuilding tradition.

Throughout the generations, when craftsmen were building wooden boats and they came to the last plank, they traditionally invited the owner of the shipyard or the vessel to be present. To show appreciation for the work being done, the owner would buy some whisky and give everybody a drink. Laying the last plank in the hull was a milestone because it marked the halfway point in the shipbuilding process. Also as part of the celebration, the owner also usually said, "Here's some money, now let's carry on."

It was a symbolic gesture, and there are variations on the tradition, one of which was to pour a small amount of whisky on the final plank. Once the last spike was driven into the plank, the tradition continued with the traditional toast to the vessel, a gesture that was said to bring good luck and safety to the vessel and to all who sailed on her.

DID YOU KNOW?

In Nova Scotia, historically Lunenburgers' drink of choice is black rum, which is traditionally splashed across the end of the plank.

More Shipbuilding Customs

☛ Shipbuilders traditionally place a silver coin under the masthead to bring the vessel good luck. Another reason is in case the sailors have to pay the ferryman when crossing the River Styx. Whenever Nova Scotians change the mast on the *Bluenose*, they also place a special coin there.

☛ It is considered bad luck for shipbuilders to be on board during the vessel's maiden voyage.

Balls on a Brass Monkey

Ever hear the saying, "Cold enough to freeze the balls off a brass monkey!"? It's pretty common in Atlantic Canada, and its explanation hearkens back to the region's seafaring heritage.

Back in the days of wooden ships, cannon balls were made of iron. They sat in a cradle beside the gun. This cradle was made of brass and had indentations in it to hold the iron cannon balls. It was called a "monkey."

Because iron and brass have different compositions, they will contract (or expand) at different rates in different temperatures. In cold temperatures, the brass contracts at a greater rate than the iron, so the balls would have a tendency to fall off the monkeys, and thus the famous saying was born.

Unique Regional Architecture

*Depending upon where you travel in Atlantic Canada,
you will encounter unique structures with their own
specific superstitions and traditions.*

LEGENDS UNDER COVER

The covered bridges of New Brunswick are world famous because of their history and beauty. The bridges have gained notoriety for many reasons, but especially for their proliferation on the provincial landscape. Dozens of these architectural wonders can be found from one end of New Brunswick to the other, including the world's longest covered bridge.

Why the Roof?

Most of New Brunswick's covered bridges were built around the start of the 20th century and are surrounded by folklore, legends and family yarns. There are several old wives' tales as to the reason the bridges were built with a cover, including the notion that such structures would protect livestock when crossing the water. Some people even went so far as to think that such bridges would scare away evil spirits. However, according to historians, the bridges were built in such a manner to protect their massive working timbers from the sun and rain. The alternate wetting and drying out of uncovered wooden structures would have resulted in rot and failure decades sooner. In fact, an uncovered wooden bridge had a life expectancy of 10 to 15 years, while a covered one could last more than 80 years.

Tunnel of Love

Known as "kissing bridges," they were a popular place to stop and sneak a hug or a kiss while courting, and it was said that any couple that had their first kiss on one of the province's covered bridges would live happily ever after. Today, hearts and names remain carved in the wood as reminders of these young lovers. Many times the horse would be so accustomed to stopping on the bridge Saturday night that it would make the same stop Sunday morning on the way to church, which would provide quite a bit of embarrassment to the young man who had been out the night before.

Bridging the Gap

☞ When you enter the bridge, if you make a wish, close your eyes, cross your fingers and hold your breath for the entire length of the bridge, your wish will come true.

☞ If you toss a coin over the side of one of the bridges and make three wishes, they will come true.

☞ If you say goodbye to a friend on a bridge, you will never see each other again.

☞ You should lift your feet off the car floor whenever you go over a bridge to keep it from falling in.

GOVERNMENT HOUSE HAS SOLE

In 2009, while extensive renovations were being undertaken on Halifax's Government House, the historic mansion that is the official residence of Nova Scotia's Lieutenant Governor, workers made an unusual discovery. Hidden inside the walls of the building were boots and shoes.

Boot Out Evil

Government House was built for Sir John Wentworth, the former Loyalist governor of New Hampshire, and his wife, Lady Frances, between 1799 and 1805. It is North America's oldest consecutively occupied government residence. When Government House was originally constructed, craftsmen in the area apparently believed that placing shoes near doors and windows warded off evil spirits at entry points, sort of acting as poltergeist scarecrows.

The tradition of putting footwear inside walls during construction was common throughout the region. In Lunenburg, homebuilders often placed a shoe or boot in the wall next to the front door in order to kick out the Devil or evil spirits.

Keeping Tradition Alive

During the recent renovations and upgrades, workers, in keeping with the old tradition, placed shoes in framed-in sections of the structure before putting up the new walls. Throughout the month of March 2009, government officials collected used footwear. Eight shoes were put into the walls of Government House, while the remainder were donated to programs that support women in transition. Meanwhile, the original shoes found in the walls were removed, catalogued and eventually returned to Government House, where they are now on permanent display.

Proudly Nova Scotian

Government House is truly a Nova Scotian creation. Building materials from around the province were used extensively, including stone from Pictou, Antigonish, Cape Breton, Lunenburg, Lockeport, Bedford Basin and the North West Arm. Pine came from the Annapolis Valley, Tatamagouche and Cornwallis. Sand was brought in from Shelburne, Eastern Passage and McNamara's Island. The bricks were from Dartmouth.

DID YOU KNOW?

When building a new house, you should always put a coin in the foundation to ensure health and happiness within the household.

Sport and Recreation

*Just like going to work, when it comes to fun and games,
Atlantic Canadians have their fair share of superstitions.*

IN THE HUNT

Hunting has been an important source of food and also recreation for Atlantic Canadians throughout the generations, and like just about everything from the region, it comes with many superstitions.

When to Go and What to Bring

☞ It is bad luck to go hunting on Sunday.

☞ You should always carry a rabbit's foot for good luck when you go hunting.

☞ It is good luck to carry raisins with you into the woods when you go hunting. It is also good luck to carry apples.

☞ It is considered bad luck to carry coins in your pocket when you go hunting.

Hunting Code of Conduct

☞ Never load your gun until you reach your hunting destination, or you will have bad luck.

☞ If you wrap black horsehair around your wrist, you will shoot straighter.

☞ If you see your shadow while you're hunting, it is bad luck and you will go home empty-handed.

☞ It is bad luck to whistle while you're hunting.

☞ It is bad luck to say the word "kill" while you're hunting.

☞ If you fire three times and miss, your hunting season is over.

☛ If you kill the first rabbit you see on your first hunting trip of the season, you will have good luck throughout the season.

☛ It is good luck to see three ducks fly over while you are hunting, but it is bad luck to shoot those ducks.

☛ You will have bad luck if you step in the paw or hoof prints of the game you are hunting.

GONE FISHING

Deep-sea fishermen and sailors are not the only ones with superstitions. In fact, those who fish in fresh water lakes and streams are equally cautious when it comes to their sport.

Head to the Fishing Hole

☛ If you fish for the first time in the season on Good Friday, good luck will follow you throughout the season.

☛ Never fish on Sunday because it will bring bad luck.

☛ Fish bite best at night during a full moon.

☛ Some people say that it is good luck to fish in the rain. Others say that the fish bite better right after a hard rain.

☛ If the cows are standing in the pasture, then it's a good day to go fishing.

Maximize Your Catch

☞ If you dig your worms before sunrise, then you will catch a greater number of fish.

☞ It is bad luck to dig your worms from your flower garden, but good luck to dig your worms from your vegetable garden.

☞ It is considered bad luck to wear black when you go fishing.

☞ It is bad luck to take a dog on a fishing trip.

☞ Fish may not bite if a barefoot woman passes you on the way to the water.

☞ It is good luck to spit on your worm after you have put it on the hook.

☞ It is unlucky to bait your hook with a worm using your left hand.

☞ It is bad luck to sit on an upturned bucket while you are out fishing.

☞ If you swear while you are fishing, you will go home empty-handed.

☞ Never whistle while you are fishing, or you will not get a bite.

☞ If you fish against the wind, you will have better luck.

☞ If you throw back the first fish you catch, then you'll be lucky for the remainder of the day.

☞ If you count the number of fish you have caught, you will catch no more for the remainder of that day. However, it is bad luck to stop fishing with an odd number of fish—without being able to count, you'll just have to hope for the best.

☛ It is unlucky to fish with your lines crossed.

☛ It is bad luck if someone steps over your fishing line.

☛ If the end of your pole touches the water, you may as well just go home because you will catch no more fish that day.

☛ Never let your shadow fall on the water while you are fishing, or you will scare away the fish.

☛ It is bad luck to change poles while fishing.

DID YOU KNOW?

It is bad luck to get married when the fish aren't biting.

BE A GOOD SPORT

People engaged in various sports are likely to be just as superstitious as anyone else.

Baseball

☛ Spitting into your hand before picking up the bat is said to bring good luck.

☛ It is good luck to stick a wad of gum on your hat.

☛ It is bad luck if a dog walks across the diamond before the first pitch.

☛ Some players believe it is good luck to step on one of the bases before running off the field at the end of an inning.

☛ It is bad luck to touch the baselines while running off and onto the field between innings.

☞ Your game will be jinxed if you lend a bat to a fellow player. However, it is good luck to lend your glove to another player.

☞ If a pitcher is throwing a perfect game or a no-hitter, do not speak to him or you'll break his luck.

Basketball

☞ The last person to shoot a basket during the warm-up will have a good game.

☞ Wipe the soles of your sneakers for good luck.

☞ Bounce the ball before taking a foul shot for good luck.

Bowling

☞ To continue a winning streak, wear the same clothes at every game.

☞ Carry charms in your bowling bag, in your pockets or around your neck for good luck.

☞ It is considered good luck to spit in your hands before picking up the bowling ball.

Golf

☞ Start only with odd-numbered clubs.

☞ Carry coins in your pockets for good luck.

Hockey

☞ It is bad luck for hockey sticks to lie crossed.

☞ It is bad luck to say "shutout" in the locker room before a game.

☛ Players believe they'll win the game if they tap the goalie on his shin pads before a game.

☛ Many players believe putting their equipment and skates on in exactly the same order before every game will give them good luck.

☛ It is bad luck for the goalie to put on his mask before going onto the ice.

Tennis

☛ It's bad luck to hold more than two balls at a time when serving.

☛ Avoid wearing the colour yellow on the court because it will give you bad luck.

☛ Walk around the outside of the court when switching sides for good luck.

☛ It is bad luck to step on the court lines.

☛ It is bad luck to lend your tennis racquet to another player.

IT'S IN THE CARDS

Avoid Bad Luck

☞ Do not play cards on Sunday because if you do, you play with the Devil, and bad luck will follow you for the entire forthcoming week.

☞ It is bad luck to drop a deck of playing cards.

☞ At one time, it was thought to be bad luck to have a dog in the same room where cards were being played.

☞ It was once thought to be bad luck to play a game of cards on a bare table. The table should always be covered.

☞ It is bad luck to whistle or sing while you're playing cards.

Play by the Rules

☞ Never take a deck of cards directly from another person's hands, or they'll pass the Devil over to you. Instead, wait for them to place the deck of cards down on the table and then pick it up.

☞ Never deal out the cards in a counter-clockwise direction.

☞ Never look at your cards until the dealer is finished.

☞ Never pick up your cards with your left hand.

☞ Never ask another player what cards they are holding.

☞ Never walk around the card table during the game.

☞ Never play for money.

☞ And finally, never, ever swear while you are playing cards, or you invoke the Devil.

Luck of the Draw

☛ Most people believe the Ace of Spades is the ultimate bad luck card because it foretells death and tragedy. In truth, the Four of Clubs, once known as the Devil's Bedpost, is just as ominous. It was considered particularly unlucky to draw that card during the first hand of any game.

☛ Some people believe that drawing a pair of red Jacks suggests that someone you are playing with is actually an enemy even if they seem like a friend.

CENTRE STAGE

Acting is one of the oldest professions in the history of humankind, so it would be natural to assume that along with the career come many superstitions.

Backstage

☛ Always leave the dressing room with your left foot first, but have visitors enter with their right foot first.

☛ Never allow another actor to look over your shoulder into the mirror while applying your makeup.

☛ It is bad luck for an actor to see his or her reflection while looking over the shoulder of another person.

☛ When applying your makeup, it is good luck to get lipstick on your teeth.

☛ Having a cat in the dressing room is good luck.

☛ It is good luck to find a piece of lint on another actor's costume.

On Stage

☞ Never open a play on the 13th day of any month.

☞ It is bad luck to say "Macbeth" in the theatre; always call it "the Scottish play."

☞ Green is not a particularly lucky colour to wear on stage.

☞ It is good luck to be pinched while on stage.

☞ It is bad luck to have real flowers on stage.

☞ It is bad luck to whistle on stage.

☞ It is bad luck to open an umbrella on stage.

Special Occasions Through the Year

Nothing brings out superstitions in Atlantic Canada like holidays and special occasions.

NEW YEAR'S

By the Stroke of Midnight...

☛ In some homes, on New Year's Eve, dishes of fresh fruit are set out as an "offering" and as a means to invite good luck into the home throughout the year.

☛ If someone gives you a coin on New Year's Eve, you should save it because it will keep giving you good luck throughout the coming year.

☛ Always sew a pillow case on New Year's Eve to hold all of your troubles and keep you from bringing them into the coming year. However, you must never leave sewing undone on New Year's Eve, or it will stay that way for the next year.

☛ It is tradition to fling open all the doors on your house at the stroke of midnight on New Year's Eve to let the old year out and to welcome in the new year.

☛ It is tradition to make lots of noise at the stroke of midnight on New Year's Eve to scare away the Devil and other evil spirits.

☛ The first person you kiss after midnight on New Year's Eve will be true to you for the next 12 months.

☛ How you start the year is how you will end it, so you must ensure that you are wearing new clothes and looking your best, have paid off all your debts and are with your partner to ensure that you are still with them at the next New Year.

☛ To ensure that you will have food throughout the coming year, make sure your cupboards are not empty when the New Year arrives.

Happy New Year

☛ If the first person to enter your house on New Year's Day has dark hair, then your household will be blessed with good luck for the next year. However, if that person has blonde or red hair, then bad luck will follow you throughout the year.

☛ The first visitor to your house in the New Year should always come bearing gifts, or there will be tragedy in that house.

☛ It is bad luck for anything to leave your house, not even the garbage, during the first day of the New Year.

☛ It is bad luck to sweep the floor on New Year's Day.

☞ You will cut off your fortune if you use scissors on New Year's Day.

☞ If you do laundry on the first day of the New Year, then it is said you are washing away the life of someone in your household, and there will surely be a death in your home within the next 12 months.

☞ It is good luck to eat cabbage for dinner on the first day of the New Year.

☞ It is good luck to wear a new piece of clothing on the first day of the New Year.

☞ Do not lend or borrow money on New Year's Day, or you will be broke for the remainder of the year.

☞ If you cry on the first day of the New Year, then it is said you will shed many tears throughout the year.

☞ To break something made of glass on New Year's Day means your heart will break by the end of the year.

☞ If the wind is calm and the weather is fine on New Year's Day, then there will be no major storms during the coming year.

☞ It is good luck to dance around a tree on New Year's Day.

☞ Babies born on January 1 are said to always have good luck.

GROUNDHOG DAY

According to North American folklore, on February 2, when a groundhog emerges from his burrow and fails to see his shadow because the weather is cloudy, then winter will soon come to an end, and winter haters say, "Hallelujah." Conversely, if the weather is sunny and the groundhog sees his shadow, he will retreat back into his burrow and stay there. Legend has it that his retreat foretells that there will be six more weeks of winter.

Then and Now

The legend of the groundhog actually dates back to the 18th century in Germany and first came to North America via Pennsylvania around 1887. Today, Groundhog Day has practically become a national holiday, with festivals, marching bands, banners and a full day of celebrations in some places.

Atlantic Canadian Groundhogs

Nova Scotians have anointed Shubenacadie Sam as their chief weather prognosticator. However, there is also the forecaster from Cape Breton known as Two Rivers Tunnel who, some followers say, has never been wrong.

Other Famous Groundhogs

Other famous Canadian groundhog meteorologists include Wiarton Willie, Gary the Groundhog and Chilly Charlie in Ontario, Brandon Bob in Manitoba and Balzac Billy in Alberta. However, the granddaddy of them all is Punxsutawney Phil from Pennsylvania, USA.

VALENTINE'S DAY

It should not come as a surprise that there are so many superstitions connected to Valentine's Day specifically, considering all the superstitions related to love and marriage.

Valentine Divinations

☛ On the eve of Valentine's Day, a maiden should take five bay leaves and pin them to her pillow, one in each corner and one in the middle. That night, she will dream of her future lover or husband.

☛ It was believed that the type of bird a woman sees fly over her head on Valentine's Day indicates the type of man she will marry:

- If she sees a robin, she will marry a sailor;

- If she sees a sparrow, she will marry a poor man but be very happy;

- If she sees a goldfinch, she will marry a millionaire;

- If she sees an owl, she will remain a spinster;

- If she sees a bluebird, she will marry a happy man;

- If she sees a blackbird, she will marry a priest or clergyman;

- And if she sees a crossbill, she will marry an argumentative man.

☞ If she sees a flock of doves on Valentine's Day, she will have a happy, peaceful marriage.

☞ If a woman sees a squirrel on Valentine's Day, she will marry a cheapskate who will hoard all their money.

Other Valentine Superstitions

☞ The first man's name an unmarried woman hears on Valentine's Day will be the name of the man she will marry.

☞ The first unmarried man an unmarried woman sees on February 14 will be her future husband.

☞ If a woman finds a glove on the road on Valentine's Day, her future beloved will have the missing glove.

☞ If a woman cuts an apple in half on Valentine's Day, the number of seeds found inside will indicate the number of children she will have.

DID YOU KNOW?

It is lucky to be awoken by a kiss on Valentine's Day.

LEAP YEAR

Leap Year is not just another ordinary year. In fact, there are many beliefs associated with the special day.

⚞⚟

Thirty days hath September, April, June and November;
All the rest have thirty-one,
Excepting February alone,
Which hath but twenty-eight, in fine,
Till leap year gives it twenty-nine.

⚞⚟

Leap Year Luck

☛ Because February 29 occurs only every four years, it is said to be lucky—anything started on that day will be successful. The exception to the rule is marriage; some people believe the marriage will fail if the wedding is held on February 29.

☛ February 29 is the only day of the year when it is permitted for a woman to propose marriage to a man. It is bad luck for the man to say no.

☛ Babies born on February 29 are said to be both lucky and extremely healthy and will go on to lead long, successful lives. Anyone born on February 29 can celebrate their birthday either on February 28 or March 1, but legally their birthday comes only every four years.

☛ As a weather predictor, if the sky is clear and bright on February 29, the next 12 months will be filled with storms.

EASTER

Easter Beliefs

☛ Crops should never be planted on Good Friday because there is an old belief that says no iron (shovel, spade, etc.) should enter the ground on this most holy of days.

☛ Eggs laid on Good Friday will never go bad.

☛ Bread or cakes baked on Good Friday will not go mouldy.

☛ Hot cross buns baked on Good Friday were said to have magical powers, along with with the fact that they won't go mouldy. Old hot cross buns are supposed to protect the house from fire. Sailors took Easter hot cross buns to sea with them to prevent shipwrecks. They were even used as medicine; a hot cross bun baked on Good Friday and left to get hard could be grated up and put in some warm milk to stop an upset stomach.

☞ Having a haircut on Good Friday will prevent toothaches the rest of the year.

☞ Just like on New Year's Day, for good luck during the year, wear new clothes on Easter Sunday, and don't do laundry on Good Friday, or you'll wash a member of your family away.

☞ A child born on Good Friday and baptised on Easter Sunday is said to have the gift of healing.

☞ The spirit of a person who dies on Good Friday will go directly to heaven.

DID YOU KNOW?

It is widely believed that if a woman knocks on your door in springtime, then bad luck will visit the house; however, if a man knocks on the door, then it is good luck.

HALLOWEEN

Trick or treat,
Smell my feet,
Give me something good to eat.

Black Magic

☛ While black cats are considered bad luck on most days, it is actually good luck for a black cat to cross your path on Halloween.

☛ If a bat flies around your house on Halloween, someone you know will soon die.

Sorcery

☛ For good luck, light a candle on Halloween, but do not burn that candle at any other time of the year.

☛ If you gaze into the flame of a lit candle on Halloween, you will see into the future.

☛ If the flame of a candle suddenly goes out by itself on Halloween, it is said that a ghost has come to visit.

DID YOU  KNOW?

A person born on Halloween is said to be able to see and speak with spirits.

Spells

☛ If an unmarried woman eats an apple on Halloween, she will be married within a year. In some versions of this superstition, the apple must be suspended on a string from the ceiling for it to work.

☛ An old Halloween game is for all the unmarried young people to fasten an apple on a string and twirl it around before a hot fire. The one whose apple falls off first will be the first to marry.

CHRISTMAS

Because Christmas is such an auspicious time of year, it's not surprising that superstitions abound.

Deck the Halls

☛ Placing holly around your house at Christmas is said to bring good luck and will also keep the witches away during the Christmas season.

☛ If your Christmas tree falls over, it means someone you know will soon die.

☛ Placing acorns on your Christmas tree will bring you good luck.

☛ Hanging a wreath on your door at Christmas is a sign of welcome to all those who will enter.

☛ It is considered good luck to keep a fire burning in your house during the 12 days of Christmas.

DID YOU KNOW?

It is bad luck to sing Christmas carols at any other time of the year.

'Tis the Season for Giving

☞ In modern times, we use Canada Post to get our letters to Santa, but in earlier times, it was a tradition to burn the Christmas letters in the fire so that they would be magically transported by the wind to the North Pole.

☞ If you plan to give a piece of clothing as a Christmas gift, do not wash it before gifting it because that washes away the good luck.

☞ In some households, it is a tradition that when it comes to opening gifts on Christmas morning, the oldest person in the home should go first, followed by the youngest. After that, the order does not matter.

The Night Before Christmas

☞ A loaf of bread left on the table after Christmas Eve dinner will ensure a steady supply of bread for the next year.

☞ It is bad luck to consume alcohol on Christmas Eve.

☞ If you eat an apple at midnight on Christmas Eve, you will have good health throughout the following year.

- Burning an old pair of shoes on Christmas Eve is said to bring you good luck.

- A clear, star-filled sky on Christmas Eve is considered good luck by farmers as it said to be a sign of a good crop in the coming summer.

- If there is no moon on Christmas Eve, the following harvest will be rich.

- If there is snow on the ground on Christmas Eve, it is said to bring good luck.

- If a dog howls on Christmas Eve, it is a sign of bad luck.

- Opening the doors of your house at midnight on Christmas Eve will allow the evil spirits to escape.

- The gender of the first person to enter your house on Christmas Eve was said to predict the sex of the child of any pregnant women in the household.

- Keeping a candle lit throughout Christmas Eve will bring good luck to your household. But it is bad luck if that candle goes out during the night.

- Placing lit candles in your windows on Christmas Eve will help guide lost loved ones back to your home.

DID YOU KNOW?

A person who dies at midnight on Christmas Eve will go straight to heaven because the gates of heaven are open at that time.

We Wish You a Merry Christmas

☞ A blowing wind on Christmas Day brings good luck with it.

☞ If a bird visits your house on Christmas Day, that is said to be good luck.

☞ Having difficulty lighting a fire on Christmas Day is a sign that you will have bad luck for the remainder of the year.

☞ It is bad luck to go fishing on Christmas Day.

☞ Never wash clothes on Christmas Day because it is bad luck, and it will cause a boat somewhere to sink.

☞ It is bad luck to wear new shoes on Christmas Day.

☞ It is considered bad luck if the first visitor to your house on Christmas Day is a woman.

DID YOU KNOW?

It is considered very lucky to be born on Christmas Eve or Christmas Day.

Eat, Drink and Be Merry

☞ The Christmas dinner table was always set for an even number of guests even it meant leaving one place unused because odd numbers were said to bring bad luck.

☞ To protect your house from burglars or intruders, tie a piece of string to the table legs where you eat your Christmas dinner.

☞ Placing a pot of honey in the centre of the Christmas dinner table is said to ward off evil spirits.

- Placing a bowl of garlic under your table for your Christmas dinner will bring you strength and protect your family throughout the coming year.

- Place fish scales under your Christmas dinner plates for good luck.

- The traditional Christmas dinner consisted of 12 courses for the 12 disciples.

- It is considered good luck to serve mince pies as part of your Christmas dinner.

- It was once believed that serving mushrooms as part of Christmas dinner would bring good fortune.

- Diners must wait at the table until everyone completes their Christmas dinner, or bad luck will befall the household.

Under the Mistletoe

- At one time, unmarried girls would steal sprigs of mistletoe from church decorations at Christmas time and hide them under their pillows because they believed doing so would cause them to dream of their future husband.

- An unmarried girl would also hang the wishbone of the Christmas fowl prongs upward over the front door. The first eligible male to enter the house before the 12th night would be her mate.

- Burning old mistletoe was said to predict the marriage prospects of an unmarried girl. Steady flames ensured a happy married life, while sputtering flames predicted a rocky union.

☞ On Christmas Day, if a virgin desires to know if she will wed within the year, she should knock on the door of a hen house at midnight. If a rooster cackles she shall, but if a hen cackles she shall not. Another method is to throw a shoe onto the roof between Christmas Day and New Year's Day; if the shoe remains on the roof and doesn't roll off, she will be married within the year.

☞ If a woman desires to know the nature of man she is dating, she should, on Christmas Day, turn her back to the woodpile and withdraw one piece of wood. Whether the wood is straight or crooked shall tell her the truth.

When it Happens in the Sky

*No matter where you travel in Atlantic Canada,
you are sure to encounter a few superstitions to explain
every weather condition known.*

WEATHER WONDERS

When the stars begin to huddle,
The earth will puddle.

Seasonal Predictions

☛ If March comes in like a lion (stormy and windy), it will go out like a lamb (calm and mild).

☛ April showers bring May flowers.

☛ If you rake your yard before the first day of April, you will bring on the rain.

☛ The old saying goes, *Ash before oak, you're in for a soak.* Ash and oak trees leaf out at different times in spring. Typically, the oak leaves appear full first, or in some years, at the same time as the ash. But if the ash leaves come out first, it means it's going to be a wet summer.

☛ A spell of unusually warm weather in the first week of August means that there will be a white winter. And if there is a cold winter, a hot summer will follow.

☛ If there is snow at Christmas, there will be a green Easter.

☛ If there is thunder in February, there will be a snowstorm in May.

DID YOU KNOW?

The sun will never shine upon a liar.

Looks Like Rain

When the dew is on the grass,
Rain will never come to pass.

☛ If the summer morning is overcast and there are plate-shaped cobwebs on the lawns, the day should turn out to be lovely and sunny.

☛ In summer, if leaves curl up so the underside is visible, it's a sign of rain.

☛ Dogs (haze) around the sun mean that it's going to rain.

☛ If a crescent moon looks like you can hang a bucket on it, that means rain.

☛ If worms come to the surface of the ground in the daytime, it will rain.

☛ If you hear a frog croaking in the daylight, it means rain is coming.

DID YOU  KNOW?

It was believed that hanging Rosary beads on the clothesline on wash day would keep the rain from coming.

Stormy Weather

- When the birds gather in large flocks in the trees, head for cover because a major storm will soon follow.

- Birds flocking together in large numbers on a winter day means a snowstorm is coming.

- If you see a bird flying during a snowstorm, brace for a major snowfall.

- If a wood fire spits at you when you put wood in, it is a sure sign of an approaching storm.

- If the smoke from a fire rises straight up, the weather will remain calm for the next 24 hours. Conversely, if the smoke lays low and spreads out, you should expect a storm within 24 hours.

No weather is ill,
If the wind is still

- A ring around the moon means that a storm is approaching—the larger the ring, the farther off the storm.

- It is said to be bad luck when there is lightning in the sky but no thunder.

Red Skies

Red sky at night,
Sailors delight;
Red sky in the morning,
Sailors take warning.

While generations of folks living in coastal communities have repeated this saying throughout the ages (it can actually be found in Shakespeare and also in the Bible in slightly different forms), there is a logical and scientific explanation for the phenomenon.

It essentially comes from the fact that in the Northern Hemisphere, weather systems typically move from west to east. If the sky is red at night (sunset), then what is producing the redness (dust, impurities in the atmosphere) is to the west. It will be an area of stable air, usually denoted by high pressure, which is a "fair-weather" producer. Therefore, that area of stable air, fair weather, will be moving towards you. If, however, the red sky is in the morning—the east—then the fair weather area of high pressure has passed by and is now to the east.

Evening red and morning grey,
Speed the traveller on his way.
Evening grey and morning red,
Bring down rain upon his head.

Rainbow at noon, more rain soon.
Rainbow in the east, sailors at peace.
Rainbow in the west, sailors in distress.
Rainbow in the morning, farmers take warning.
Rainbow at night, farmers' delight.

Lightning Lore

☞ Never stand under a tree in a lightning storm.

☞ Never open an umbrella when there is lightning.

☞ Never stand in a water puddle in the middle of a lightning storm.

☞ Never stand in high places in the middle of a lightning storm.

☛ Never wear red clothing in a lightning storm.

☛ Never sit on a toilet in the middle of a lightning storm.

☛ Never stand by a window during a lightning storm.

☛ Never turn on a light switch during a lightning storm.

☛ Never plug in or unplug an electrical appliance in the middle of a lightning storm.

☛ You should cover mirrors during a lightning storm because they are thought to attract lightning.

☛ Placing an acorn in a window will prevent lightning from entering your house.

The sharper the blast,
The sooner it's past.

Snow Day

☛ If you burn leaves in the fall, snow follows.

☛ If the first snow of the winter is subsequently washed away by rain, then the remainder of the winter will be open with little snowfall.

☛ In Newfoundland, they say that if the dogberry trees are laden with berries, it means a lot of winter snow.

☛ When there are lots of holly berries and pinecones, anticipate a winter with lots of snow.

☛ If an early snow sticks to the sides of trees, expect a long, cold winter.

☛ If there are two circles around a full moon, it is sign that it will snow within the next 24 hours.

☛ It is said that if children wear their pajamas backwards, there will be a major snowstorm overnight and school will be cancelled the next day. Children can also try sleeping with their feet at the head of the bed and their head at the foot, as it is said that doing so may also bring on a major snowstorm.

See how high the hornets nest,
'twill tell how high the snow will rest.

DID YOU KNOW?

Dreaming of snow is usually good luck.

Onion skins thick and tough,
Coming winter cold and rough.

The Three Snows

It's a common belief in Nova Scotia's Annapolis Valley—the apple-growing capital of Atlantic Canada—that there are always three snowfalls after the equinox in March before it is truly spring. So reliable is this that the "Three Snows" have names: Smelt Snow, Robin Snow and Grass Snow. The first snow coincides with the smelt migration on rivers; the second with the first robins appearing in spring; and the third is known as poor man's fertilizer.

Year of snow,
Fruit will grow.

Size Matters

There is an old saying in Atlantic Canada that goes:

Little snow, big snow;
Big snow, little snow.

One often hears this statement at the start of a snowfall, in reference to the size of the flakes. The scientific explanation for this phenomenon would be that the larger flakes are falling from the type of cloud that produces flurries—a convective type of cloud (summertime showers)—and in passing any one spot would not necessarily produce a great snowfall.

The reason the flakes are larger is that the upward and downward motion of air within this type of cloud is great enough to cause the flakes to join together. They are held in suspension within the cloud until they are too heavy to be kept up by these updrafts, and they fall to earth. This is not to say that you will not get a lot of snow from "flurries"—lines of them sometimes develop and can produce snow squalls. But generally, flurries come and go and are of shorter duration.

The smaller flakes come from the type of cloud that does not have as great or as many updrafts and downdrafts and therefore can fall as the water vapour develops them into snowflakes.

BY THE LIGHT
OF THE MOON

Moonlight Madness

☞ It was once thought that if you went outside during a lunar eclipse, you would become senile.

☞ Sleeping in direct moonlight causes madness or blindness.

☞ Crazy people come out on the full moon of the month.

☞ It is good luck to bow to the moon when you first see it in the evening.

☞ It was once thought unlucky to look at a new moon through a window:

See the new moon through the glass,
You'll have sorrow while it lasts.

☞ Looking at the new moon over your right shoulder will bring you good luck.

☞ If a baby is born on a moonless night, he or she will not live to reach puberty.

☞ A wish made on a new moon will come true sometime within the next 12 months.

Moon Meteorology

☞ When there is fog and a small moon in the same night, a strong wind will follow.

☞ If the moon is red, there will be a strong wind.

☞ When the moon is low, the tides will be higher than normal.

☛ If a new moon occurs on a Saturday, there will be 20 days of wind and rain.

☛ If a new moon occurs on a Sunday, there will be a flood before the month is out.

☛ If the new moon is on a Monday, the weather will be good.

☛ The worst storms are likely to occur one to three days after a new moon and three to five days after a full moon.

Clear moon,
Frost soon.

Names of the Full Moon

The full moon is tied to many local superstitions, but did you know that each full moon of every month has its own name?

☛ January: Wolf Moon or Old Moon as the New Year begins.

☛ February: Snow Moon or Hunger Moon because the snow is typically heavier at this time of year, and hunting is more difficult.

☛ March: Worm Moon because as the frost begins to leave the ground, the worms begin to appear. Also known as the Sap Moon because the maple sap begins to flow.

☛ April: Pink Moon, Egg Moon or Fish Moon because with the arrival of spring, the fish are starting to run in the rivers and lakes.

☛ May: Flower Moon or Planting Moon because this is the month when gardens spring to life.

☛ June: Strawberry Moon, Rose Moon or Hot Moon because it's the time of the summer solstice.

☛ July: Buck Moon as bucks begin to grow new antlers, or Thunder Moon for the summer storms.

☛ August: Sturgeon Moon because it is said that more sturgeon were caught during this full moon than at any other time of the year. Also known as Grain Moon.

☛ September: Corn Moon because of the corn harvest. Also known as Barley Moon.

☛ October: Harvest Moon because this is the full moon nearest the fall equinox.

☛ November: Beaver Moon as this was traditionally the time of year when beaver traps were set before the waterways froze. Also known as Frost Moon.

☛ December: Cold Moon or Long Nights Moon as this is when winter begins.

Pale moon doth rain;
Red moon doth blow;
White moon doth neither rain nor snow.

Lucky Miscellanea

*Ever wonder why some people seem to have more
bad luck than good luck? This may help.*

A DOSE OF BAD LUCK

As they say in Atlantic Canada, if a series of misfortunes fall upon you, then you're having a run of bad luck. Thankfully, you can change your luck by turning three times counter clockwise.

⚜

Sing in the street, disappointment you'll meet.
Sing before seven, you'll cry before eleven.
If you sing before you eat, you'll cry before you sleep.
Sing while eating or sing in bed,
Evil will get you and you'll be dead.

⚜

Household Hazards

☛ When visiting another's home, it is considered bad luck to pour your own drink. It is also a sign that you are unimportant and not prosperous if you have to pour your own drink. To have someone pour your drink indicates that you have friends who want to share their drinks with you.

☛ You should always leave a house by the same door you entered, or bad luck will follow you for the next 24 hours.

☛ You should never shake hands with someone in a doorway, or you and the other person will eventually become enemies.

☛ It is bad luck to open an umbrella inside. One theory as to why suggests that an umbrella protects you against the storms of life, so opening one in your house insults the guardian spirits of your home, causing them to leave you unprotected.

☛ It is bad luck to whistle inside your house. Some people believe it will cause you to lose all your money. Others believe that by whistling inside, you are inviting death to come calling, and someone in the household will soon die.

☛ You should always get out of bed on the same side that you got in, or you will have bad luck. You should also get out of bed with your left foot first.

☛ It is bad luck for two people to make a bed at the same time.

☛ It is bad luck when two people pass on a set of stairs. However, it can also be a sign that a wedding is in the future of one these people.

☛ It is bad luck to leave a hairbrush on a table.

☛ If you drop a comb while you are combing your hair, it means you are in for disappointment.

DID YOU KNOW?

When you find a hairpin, press the ends together. If the ends are even, you will meet a boy; if uneven, you will meet a girl.

Furthermore, it is bad luck:

☛ To close a pocketknife opened by someone else.

☛ To see a bat in the middle of the day.

☛ If your chair falls over when you get up.

☛ To bring an axe into your home.

- To throw a gift away.

- To swing an empty swing.

- To rock an empty rocking chair.

- To cut your finger or toe nails on Sunday.

- To point your finger at the sun.

- To light a cigarette with a candle.

- To turn back for anything after you have set out to go anywhere.

- To leave your feet on the floor of your vehicle whenever you drive over railway tracks.

Strict Calendar Rules

- If you hang a new calendar before January 1, you will be faced with a full year of bad luck.

☛ It is also bad luck to turn the page of a calendar to a new month before the old month is out, and bad luck when you do not turn the page on the first day of the new month before noon.

Ladders Are Not Lucky

☛ If you walk under a ladder, you will have bad luck. An open ladder forms a triangle, and because triangles were once considered a symbol of life and the Holy Trinity, walking through that shape is tempting your fate.

☛ It is bad luck to pass a flag through the rungs of a ladder.

Seven Years of Bad Luck

It is said that when you break a mirror, you will endure seven years of bad luck unless you can find a way to counteract the negative effects. The origin of this superstition can be traced back to the Romans, who were the first to create glass mirrors. They and other early cultures believed that a mirror had the power to confiscate part of the user's soul. If the user's reflected image became distorted in any way, this could mean a corruption of the soul. If the user should break a mirror, it would mean his or her soul would be trapped inside the mirror.

Essentially, a broken mirror created a broken soul, which in turn led to the broken health of the unfortunate user. The Romans also believed that a person's physical body renewed itself every seven years, so under that criteria, it would take seven years before the user's soul would be fully restored. Up until then, life for a mirror breaker would be one long string of unfortunate events because he or she no longer had a healthy soul to ward off spiritual evil-doers.

Fortunately, there are also a number of rituals said to counteract the very bad hair day created when you break a mirror. Because the pieces of the mirror can still reflect the corrupted soul, the entire mirror should be ground into dust—no reflection, no problem. In Atlantic Canada, it is also suggested that after you break a mirror, you should bury the pieces under a tree during a full moon.

More Mirror Mishaps

☞ Another superstition for breaking a mirror was that shortly thereafter, a family member would die.

☞ It is bad luck to see your face in a mirror by candlelight.

☞ It is bad luck for two people to look into a mirror simultaneously.

WHEN LADY LUCK SMILES

If you think people in Atlantic Canada are superstitious when it comes to omens of bad luck, then check out these beliefs that encourage good luck.

Lots o' Luck!

☞ Yellow is the colour for good luck.

☞ Dreaming of angels is a sign of success and happiness.

☞ Carry a rabbit's foot in your pocket for good luck. The belief that carrying a rabbit's foot around with you will bring you good luck can be traced as far back as the seventh century BCE, when the rabbit was considered a talismanic symbol, and carrying the left hind foot was a handy way to benefit from the rabbit's luck.

☞ A horseshoe nail is frequently used as a good luck charm if it is bent into a circle by a blacksmith. Carry it with you at all times.

☞ To ensure good luck, health and safety on a trip, you should sit on your suitcase once it is packed. Then just before leaving, you should take one last look in the mirror.

☞ If you find a sand dollar on the beach, you should take it home and put it in your garden for good luck.

☞ Picking up a pencil in the street is said to be good luck.

☞ Counting the cars on a train is said to give you good luck.

☞ Finding nine peas in a pea pod is a sign of good fortune.

Lucky Oak

☛ To protect their houses from vengeful lightning strikes, it is said the Ancient Norse would fill their homes with acorns collected from northern oak forests. Today, many people still carry an acorn in their pocket for good luck.

☛ Knock three times on wood if speaking of something that might bring good fortune or to prevent bad luck. The idea of touching or knocking on wood for good luck stems from ancient beliefs that oak trees possessed special powers, and in fact, the oak tree was considered the tree of life.

DID YOU KNOW?

If acorns appear in your dreams, that is a sign of good luck.

Cheers!

☛ When opening a bottle and pouring a drink for someone else, you should first pour a little into your own glass for good luck and good health.

☛ Leaving the last mouthful of rum in the bottle will bring you good luck. Giving the bottle to a friend will double the luck.

☛ It is good luck to spill wine while proposing a toast. In the old days, spilling wine (or beer) from one glass to another during a toast was done deliberately to show that the wine was not poisoned and that the guest had nothing to fear from the host.

☛ In some areas of Atlantic Canada, when drinking outside it is considered good luck and good manners to pour several drops directly onto the ground. This is also a way to remember your dead friends, who can then share a drink with you. This is often done amongst sailors who remember their dead brethren by dumping rum into the ocean so that those who have perished at sea can share a drink with them.

Four Leaves of Luck

☛ A four-leaf clover is said to bring good luck:

One leaf for fame,
And one leaf for wealth;
One for a faithful lover,
And one to bring you glorious health
Are all in a four leaf clover.

☛ Finding a five-leaf clover is even luckier than finding a four-leaf clover.

WISH I MAY, WISH I MIGHT

When to Wish

☞ If you wish upon the first star you see in the evening, it is said your wish will come true. The same holds true for wishing upon a falling star.

☞ If you find a loose eyelash, you should place it on the back of your hand and lightly blow it off while making a wish.

☞ If two people say the same thing at the same time, they should touch something black and make a wish.

☞ If you ever find yourself between two people who have the same name, you should make a wish.

☞ When you taste something for the first time, make a wish, and that wish will come true.

DID YOU KNOW?

Crossing your fingers is a near-universal sign of wishing for something. One theory about its origin is that when Christianity was illegal, crossing fingers was a secret way for Christians to recognize each other.

Wishing on a Stone

A wishing stone is a stone or pebble found on the seashore. Legend says that in order for it to be a true wishing stone, it must have a white quartz ring on it somewhere. The ring must be complete, with no breaks or pauses in the circle it forms. The ring can be crossed by other rings, but must have no beginning and no end in order for the magic to work.

Wishing stones are popular in most seaside provinces, but they are especially revered in coastal communities throughout Nova Scotia, where it is believed that if you keep a wishing stone in your pocket, it will eventually make all your wishes come true.

However, according to legend, when you find a wishing stone, you should stand by the water's edge, hold the stone in your hand, close your eyes and make a silent wish. Once you have made a wish, throw the stone as far into the sea as you can, and your wish will come true.

MONEY MAKES THE WORLD GO 'ROUND

Just like most everything else in Atlantic Canada, money has its own fair share of superstitions.

Signs of Fortune

☛ When a cup of coffee is poured, if it foams or bubbles on the top, it is a sign that you will soon be coming into money. In order to secure your wealth, you should take a spoon and scoop as much of the "money" out of the cup as you can before taking a drink.

☛ If a bird poops on your head, it is a sign from heaven that you will soon come into money. This belief is based on the feeling that when you suffer an inconvenience (albeit a pretty gross one), you've earned some sort of reward.

☛ If you find a floating feather, you will soon come into money.

☛ If you have money in your pocket when you hear the first peepers in spring, then you will have money all year. Or, an alternate version says that if you have money in your pocket on New Year's Eve, then you'll have money throughout the coming year.

DID YOU KNOW?

It's thought that random dimes lying around are supposed to be tokens left by your loved ones in heaven to let you know they are watching over you.

Money Dos and Don'ts

☛ It is bad luck to gift an empty purse or wallet to someone else. You should always make sure it contains money, even if it is just a nickel, or the recipient will always be broke.

☛ Never leave your pockets, purses or wallets completely empty, and never completely empty your bank account. Always leave at least a coin or two to replenish your funds.

☛ You should never pay out money on Sunday, or you will be paying it out all week. Another version has it that you should never pay out money on Monday, or you will be broke for the entire week.

☛ There is a widely held belief that you should never lend money to a friend, as it's a sure-fire way to ruin a friend-ship. However, if you feel you must lend your friend money, then it's better to lend the money in small amounts over different times rather than in one large sum at one time. This allows the bad luck to diminish in between lendings.

☞ If you are buying something with cash, you should always try to give the money with your right hand and take the change with your left hand. Doing so will improve your financial situation.

☞ If you burn the peelings from an onion, it is said you will always have money.

☞ It is bad luck to pick up a coin if it is tails side up. It is good luck if it is heads up.

☞ It is bad luck to throw money in a fire.

☞ If you throw a penny away, it will come back to you ten-fold.

☞ Throw a penny over your right shoulder into a lake, and it will bring you good luck.

☞ If you find a penny, give it away to someone for good luck.

☞ If you find a penny on the ground, you should pick it up, rub it on your bum cheek and put it in your shoe so it will bring you good luck. Some people believe that this only works if you put it in your left shoe. Others believe the shoe must correspond with the hand you used to retrieve the penny.

See a penny, pick it up,
All day long you'll have good luck!
See a penny, let it lie,
All day long you'll have to cry.

BY THE NUMBERS

People in Atlantic Canada have lots of superstitions centring around numbers.

Bad Luck Runs in Threes

One of the most prevalent superstitions in Atlantic Canada suggests that bad luck comes in threes. Perhaps the reason for it is that the number three is associated with the Holy Trinity. To make a mundane use of three was to defile the sanctity of the trinity.

☛ If there is one death in the neighbourhood, two more will surely follow.

☛ Some people believe that if three people are photographed together, the person in the middle will be the first to die.

☛ If you try to light three consecutive matches with no luck, then that means something bad is about to happen.

☛ It is bad luck to light three cigarettes with the same match. A possible explanation of the origin of the superstition is that British soldiers, entrenched against Dutch foes in the Boer War, learned by bitter experience of the danger of lighting three cigarettes from one match. When the men thriftily used one match to serve three of them, they gave the Boer sniper time to spot the light, take aim and fire, killing the third man. Talk about bad luck.

Other (Un)Lucky Numbers

☛ The number seven has long been considered a number of luck, wealth and power.

☛ People with seven letters in their name will be successful.

☞ Anyone born on the seventh day of the seventh month was considered to possess special abilities such as the gift of prophecy and communicating with spirits.

☞ One of the most widespread superstitious beliefs is that the number 13 is unlucky. Many hotels and office buildings around the world do not have a room number 13 or a 13th floor.

☞ It is considered bad luck to have 13 guests at the dinner table. Try to invite one more person to dinner.

☞ It is believed that if 13 people are photographed together, one of those 13 will soon die.

☞ The belief that bad luck will prevail on Friday the 13th is the most widely held superstition in the world. It is both feared and celebrated around the globe and has been shunned and embraced throughout history and by many cultures. Some historians believe that this fear in Christians could have something to do with the fact that the Crucifixion took place on a Friday and that there were 13 men (the 12 disciples and Jesus) at the Last Supper. People afflicted with a morbid, irrational fear of Friday the 13th are said to suffer from paraskevidekatriaphobia.

☞ Many people revere the number 12 because of the 12 apostles of Christ.

☞ The number 666 is feared by some because it said to the sign of the Devil.

Something Evil This Way Comes

There's an old Maritime superstition that claims if you set an empty rocking chair rocking, you invite evil spirits to occupy the empty seat. That's just one of the many superstitions in the Atlantic region that deals with evil spirits, witches and the Devil.

EVIL SPIRITS

Evil Spirit Basics

☞ Whistling in the dark will bring evil spirits.

☞ By making a cross with your fingers, you drive away evil spirits.

☞ It is said that lit candles in the room of a dying person keep evil spirits away. Only once the person has died should you blow out the candles.

☞ If you have a ghost or evil spirit in your house, you can smoke it from your home with sweet grass.

☞ In earlier generations, when a person was leaving a house and they had a bad feeling or a "haunting," as they called it, they would wipe their feet as they were leaving the house so the spirit would not follow them.

☞ Cyclists believe that hanging a bell from their handlebars will collect the evil spirits. They also believe it is bad luck to buy your own bell.

WITCHES

Keeping Witches Out

☞ To keep a witch from entering your home, lay a broom handle across your threshold. A witch will not cross over it. If she did, she would not be able to practice witchcraft.

☞ If you bury a knife under your doorstep, a witch will not cross your threshold because she does not like cold steel. Similarly, you could lay a pair of scissors at the threshold of a door with the points facing outward.

☞ If you think your house is being visited by a witch, putting a hairpin in the top corners of your doorways will keep the witch away. If you don't have a hairpin, a fork in each corner will work the same magic.

☞ If you place a mirror at your front door, a witch will see her reflection and will not enter. This is also said to work on the Devil.

☞ Hang a reflective bulb in your window; if a witch sees her reflection, she will flee. This is called a witch's ball.

☞ Placing needles around the house is also a good way to fend off witches.

☞ If you sprinkle salt around your garden, a witch will not enter.

☞ Plant rosemary by your doorstep to keep witches from entering your home.

☞ Hanging crosses or animal horns in the trees around your property will keep witches at bay.

Further Protection from Witches

☞ Witches, seeking to control and influence their victims, were said to brew potions with collected fingernail clippings. The truly superstitious burn or bury their clippings to keep them from falling into a witch's hands.

☞ To protect yourself from witches, you should always wear blue because witches do not like blue.

☞ Bringing clover into your house will protect you from witches.

☞ It is said that witches hate brass, so to prevent a witch from making your cow's milk dry up, hang a brass bell around the animal's neck.

☞ Placing mercury in the barn will protect the animals from the powers of a witch.

☞ Burning horse or dog hair is said to be a good way to repel witches.

☞ The sound of a bell ringing will drive away a witch. This is also said to be true of evil spirits.

Sensing Witches

☛ Dogs are extremely sensitive to witches, and if they bark uncontrollably at someone, she just might be a witch.

☛ It was once thought that people with freckles, red hair or odd coloured eyes were witches.

☛ If your butter turns sour, you have been cursed by a witch.

THE DEVIL

Meeting the Devil

☛ Drinking water and looking into a mirror at midnight allows you to see the Devil.

☛ If you meet a cat at midnight, you may also meet the Devil.

☛ If you cut your finger or toe nails on Sunday, the Devil will follow you around for an entire week.

Keeping the Devil at Bay

☛ If you cross over a body of water, the Devil cannot cross after you. There are stories where a horse pulling a wagon is spooked and races forward but settles after crossing a bridge, presumably because the Devil was left behind on the other side.

☛ Some people fasten horseshoes over their doors for good luck. To keep the Devil from entering your house, hang the horseshoe upside down.

☛ If you place a mirror at your front door, the Devil will see his reflection and will not enter. This was also said to work on witches.

☛ If you paint your door blue, the Devil will not enter.

☛ In the town of Lunenburg, people built the front of their houses identical to the back so that the Devil wouldn't know which end was the front and could not enter.

Salty Protection

☛ Of course, everyone knows to throw salt over their shoulder to ward off bad luck, but apparently, the real reason for doing it is to throw salt into the eyes of the Devil.

☛ Putting salt on the doorstep of a new house will keep the Devil from entering.

☛ You can chase away the Devil if you throw salt in a fire.

The Lucky Horseshoe

One of the more widely recognized and revered good luck charms in the Atlantic region is the horseshoe. Horseshoes are made from iron, a good-luck metal, and they are crescent-shaped like the moon, which is a sign of prosperity. In most barns throughout rural communities (and even in some homes), it is customary to affix a horseshoe over the door to bring about good luck. The horseshoe must be hung with the points up to keep the luck from spilling out.

DID YOU KNOW?

A horseshoe hung in the bedroom will keep nightmares away.

Lucky Horseshoe Origins

There are many theories as to the origin of the horseshoe superstition, but most involve the age-old battle between good and evil. One story that dates back hundreds of years has it that a blacksmith in the "Old Country" encountered the Devil at his door. The Devil wanted to be shod.

Upon recognizing the Evil One, the blacksmith tied him up and went to work, inflicting great pain on his visitor. The

Devil screamed for mercy, and the blacksmith released him, but only after the Devil promised to never again enter a home protected by a horseshoe.

Another theory suggests that witches rode broomsticks because they were deathly afraid of horses. Therefore, a horseshoe is a good protective charm against witches.

THE OLD HAG OF NEWFOUNDLAND

Dark Lore

Legend has it that it happens when all things dark and evil happen—the middle of the night, naturally. What you thought was a peaceful night's sleep turns into a waking nightmare, and you find yourself pinned and unable to move, shocked awake and paralyzed by an overwhelming sense of evil. In some places, but especially in Newfoundland, they say that when it happens, it means the Old Hag has paid you visit.

While some skeptics quickly dismiss the phenomenon as your typical, everyday urban legend, the curious thing about "Old Hag syndrome" is that it is a highly reported phenomenon from around the world, suggesting there is more to this story than your typical superstition or old wives' tale. Down through the generations have been countless reports from people around the world who have claimed, at one time or another, to have woken up in terror, paralyzed. However, their reports not only include sleep paralysis, but often also seeing or hearing strange things, such as eyes in the darkness or heavy footsteps. Some witnesses report seeing a dark figure looming over their body.

Although variations of the story are present throughout the world, the Old Hag in particular finds its origins in Newfoundland folklore. Tales told of an old witch maliciously sitting on the chest of her victims while they lay in bed, or curses placed upon unsuspecting individuals, causing them to meet this terror in the night.

SOMETHING EVIL THIS WAY COMES

What's Really Going On?

Logically, the "curse" could be an actual case of sleep paraly-sis, which typically occurs when entering or coming out of REM sleep. A person may become caught in a state between sleep and consciousness, during which they remain aware of their surroundings but are unable to move. Furthermore, it's true that the prevailing sense of evil, or the alleged noises, that accompany the Old Hag could be nothing more than hallucinations occurring in that state of half-dreaming.

However, that does not explain the people who have reported similar experiences *without* the paralysis, nor the commonality of every reporting. And why, of all the possible hallucinations we could experience, do we sense evil?

Scientists and paranormal enthusiasts may be at odds about what causes the Old Hag syndrome, but one simple truth may be enough to keep you up at night—whatever the cause, it *does* exist.

ABOUT THE ILLUSTRATORS

Roger Garcia

Roger Garcia is a self-taught freelance illustrator who works in acrylics, ink and digital media. His illustrations have been published in humour books, children's books, newspapers and educational material.

When Roger is not at home drawing, he can be seen facilitating cartooning workshops at various elementary schools, camps and local art events. Roger also enjoys participating with colleagues in art shows, painting murals in schools and public places.

Peter Tyler

Peter is a graduate of the Vancouver Film School Visual Art and Design, and Classical animation programs. Though his ultimate passion is in filmmaking, he is also intent on developing his draftsmanship and storytelling, with the aim of using those skills in future filmic misadventures.

Patrick Hénaff

Born in France, Patrick Hénaff is mostly self-taught and is a versatile artist who has explored a variety of mediums under many different influences. He now uses primarily pen and ink to draw and then processes the images on computer. He is particularly interested in the narrative power of pictures and tries to use them as a way to tell stories.

Craig Howrie

Craig is a self-taught artist. His line art has been used in local businesses' private events as well as a local comic book art anthology. He is also a songwriter working feverishly at a project to see the light of day hopefully within the next decade or so....

ABOUT THE AUTHOR

Vernon Oickle

Bestselling author Vernon Oickle is an international award-winning journalist and editor with 33 years experience working in community newspapers on Nova Scotia's South Shore. Among his many awards for writing and photography is the Golden Quill Award for best editorial writing from the International Society of Weekly Newspaper Editors. He won the award in 2012 and is only the third Canadian and the first Nova Scotian to win the honour since it was first presented in 1961. In addition to his newspaper career, he is the author of 21 books. Vernon and his wife Nancy have two sons, Kellen and Colby. He continues to reside in Liverpool, where he was born and raised.